Who is Talking Out of My Head?

GRIEF AS AN
OUT OF BODY EXPERIENCE

by Jocelyn Faire

Produced by:

FriesenPress

Suite 300 – 852 Fort Street
Victoria, BC, Canada V8W 1H8

www.friesenpress.com

Distributed to the trade by The Ingram Book Company

TABLE OF CONTENTS

This book is lovingly dedicated to the memory of

Jordan David Isaac

Brittany Jane Marie

All the days ordained for me were written in your book
before one of them came to be.
— Psalm 139:16 NIV

I am privileged to be called your mother.

PREAMBLE

Welcome....

To those of you reading this story who have been involved in my journey as supporting cast, I wish to thank you, tremendously.

If you are reading this book, you are likely involved in the process of grief, or know someone who has undergone serious loss. Very few of us will escape tragedy of some form as we navigate through life.

This book was written using my journals and the emotions and thoughts that were experienced at the time. This is about the *raw* and *honest* reactions that accompanied my grief. This is not about trying to sugarcoat the story to spare feelings. No offence is meant for anyone; the writing of this book has come with another bucket of tears.

His grace will cover a multitude of situations.

I thank the many people who have supported me in this journey of grief and recovery, those of you who have cried with me and prayed with, or for me and our family ... you know who you are, some of you I have not even met.

As my daughter Kristen, has said many times, *"The final chapters have not been written."*

I thank you Kristen for such great support and understanding.

And thank you, Kevin, for supporting and loving Kristen so well. Together you have increased my joy in having such delightful grandchildren.

Thank you to Ralph, you encouraged me to tell this difficult story.

To my family, especially my siblings and sister-in-law, my mother; you have been the strength on which I was able to move ahead.

To many friends who walked alongside.

Thank-you to Caroline, Crystal, Dorothy and Rita for editing assistance, and encouragement.

Above all else, I Thank God. You allowed me to rail, question, shout and weep. You held my hand. I could not have lived had You not helped me to breathe.

To those of you reading .... I suggest you get some Kleenex as you start.

A note of explanation, journal entries have been marked with *** *entry.* ***

For the most part, they have been left as is, minor changes made to clarify the sentences.

Unless poems are otherwise acknowledged, they are my writings.

Front Cover artwork by Kristen Naomi, my daughter. (The concept came from a painting I purchased in New Zealand by an artist Chris B at a local craft market—I was unable to track her down)

Scriptures marked NIV are: Scripture Quotations taken from the HOLY BIBLE, NEW INTERNATIONAL VERSION, copyright © 1973, 1978, 1984 by International Bible Society.

Scriptures marked as MSG are: "Scripture taken from *THE MESSAGE.* Copyright © 1993, 1994, 1995, 1996, 2000, 2001, 2002. Used by permission of NavPress Publishing Group."

CHAPTER ONE

THE BEGINNING OF THIS STORY

"Are you Jocelyn Fehr?"

I was about to dismiss the caller as another one of those telemarketers, because he did not know how to pronounce my name....but hesitantly said, "Yes," thinking that I wanted to hang up already.

"Is Jordan Fehr your son?"

Now my heart began to beat more quickly. "Yes."

"Well, he's been in an accident....I'm so and so calling from the Victoria hospital."

I was afraid to ask, but did, "How serious?"

"Critical."

That phone call marked the beginning of a descent into hell.

My hands were shaking badly and my mind was going in a million directions as I called Ralph, and told him the news that Jordan had been in an accident. It was Sunday February 27, 2005, early evening. Ralph had gone back to work, after we'd sent our youngest daughter Brittany, our son Jordan and his girlfriend Jamie off to Winnipeg, about an hour and a half away. The plan was for Jordan and Jamie to drive Britt to the airport to catch her flight to Calgary, and then they were headed to see Jamie's parents. The previous night, we'd come back from a two-week missions trip to Queretero, Mexico. It had been an incredible time of stretching ourselves physically, emotionally, and spiritually as we participated hands on in the construction of an orphanage in Mexico! Three hours earlier we had fuelled up Jordan's white Honda Accord, taken farewell pictures at the gas pumps, hugged them and they were off.

Just before the phone call, I had come back from a walk on which I'd been reflecting on our time away and what new directions and possibilities seemed to stem from the Spanish adventure. It had been obvious to the group that love had been blossoming between Jordan and the amazing female who sang the '*Hallelujah*' song, with goose-bump inspiring vocals. The second last evening in Mexico, after the day of bricks and mortar, mixing concrete, shovelling piles of rock and gravel, the amazing duo entertained their co-workers with a busking session under the Mexican stars. Oh, love was in the air, as they sang to each other, "*You're safe and sound with me.*"

Brittany had connected so well with the children there. Her ready smile and eagerness to jump in and get involved through games, crafts and faltering Spanish, had won the hearts of most of the young girls she encountered. She had also spoken to the director as she was eager to see if she could return as a staff member in the fall. (Her dad and I wondered—What about your studies?") Oh, it had been so pleasant to have the sense that things were heading in a very good direction for all of us.

But for now, we were speeding to Winnipeg on icy roads. We had not really been aware of the icy roads. *Why Lord had we not known?* As we had travelled back from Grand Forks the night before, it had been icy on the Interstate highway, but somehow with the sunshine of the day, it seemed the perfectly logical thing to do, to send them on their way. They all needed to get back to their lives.

Frantic I tried to call people to ask them to pray for us as we sped toward the city. It seemed no one was home, or I couldn't remember their numbers as I dialled. I left a few desperate pleas for prayer on some answering machines, stating that Jordan had been in an accident and we were en route to the hospital. Finally, I got through to my mother and I asked her to call my brother Curtis and his wife Debbie. The message came back that Curt and Debbie were going to meet us at the hospital.

As we'd been driving, I kept repeating Psalm 121. "I lift up my eyes to the hills—where does my help come from? ... My help comes from the Lord." Driving as fast as we dared it was as though we were being transported into an unreal world. Ralph was voicing his concerns that Jordan would be a paraplegic or crippled for the rest of his life. We could not voice our worst fears. From then on, it was as if we were on the outside looking in.

Speeding through an intersection we saw the speed-camera flash go off and thought, I guess we'll get a ticket, but who cares? At the moment, we were focused on getting to the hospital as soon as possible. As we pulled in to Victoria hospital, there were only paid parking spots and Ralph wanted to go in first to get money to pay for the ticket. I said, "Forget it, let's go."

We ran up the hospital steps into a nightmare.

Surreal.

"Please, please, God, don't have us being escorted into a little room to tell us bad news, please."

That was my plea. "Please don't take us into a little room."

Out of breath and frantic, I explained to the enquiry person that we'd received a call, and that we couldn't get a proper parking ticket. The lady tried to maintain her composure and told us she'd take us into a room where someone would come and give us a further explanation. My heart cried out: "*NO GOD. I don't want to go into a little room.*" We got a call that Curt and Deb were on their way. Where should they meet us?

From that moment life moved in slow motion: I could see us walking down the corridor; actors in a B-grade, black and white movie, with other people in the seats of the waiting room. There was sound and commotion, but the volume switch had been turned down. I did not hear anything above the pounding of my heart and the pleas to stop taking us into that room. People in the waiting room.

Waiting....

Waiting, waiting.... It seemed to take forever until a female chaplain walked in. She paused, took in a deep breath and gave us the news that Jordan had been killed in a car accident.

"NOooooo, Noooo, NO." I cried out, I groaned.

"No, not Jordan." It took about two minutes.

Then Ralph asked "There were three people in the car. What happened to Jamie and Brittany?"

Another long pause.

"I'm so, so sorry, sir; they were all killed."

"NO!!!!" My world crashed in around me.

"I will take you to see him."

NO! NO, this could not be happening.

We were escorted to view Jordan ... Again it became an out of body experience. People turned to look at us as if they all knew something horrible had occurred, some kind of great loss. I could see in their eyes sympathy and relief that they were not the ones being escorted into that room of tragedy. That tragedy was the reason they were all waiting.

The doctors had been tied up dealing with this accident, and they were glad for the moment that they had been spared ... they were just waiting, and in some deeper sense, they were happy to wait, because they were going to be all right. Those people who got escorted *to the room*, they were the suffering ones tonight.

We were brought into a small room with a curtain. The curtain was pulled back....

Jordan, my beautiful Jordan David Isaac ... lying there ... Just a few hours ago, we had hugged him and said goodbye after what had been such a wonderful trip of a lifetime!!

And now, here he was. Cold. All the life out of his body.

"He was so full of goodness, Lord. How and *Why, why, why*????"

The female RCMP officer at the scene had picked up his Bible and it was placed here on the table beside his still and colorless body.

"Oh, God. Help us, hold me up."

In the blur of this all, we were escorted back to *the room*, where Curtis and Debbie met us. They just hugged us and cried with us, and then they took on the role of helping us to walk. Somewhere, someone slipped a note to us that said, "All of Winkler is praying for you."

Word had gotten back to our hometown of about 8,000 people of our tragedy and people had started to pray. Mildred, mother of our son-in-law, was contacted and asked to notify our daughter Kristen, who was studying with her husband Kevin in Africa.

In the midst of the blur, as we waited to meet Jordan's girlfriend's parents at the hospital, the Lord gave me a thought. I shared it with Ralph, to say, "Whatever happens, we cannot be putting the blame of this accident on anyone." This was as much for me as for him, for all the *what ifs*. *What if* we'd driven them to Winnipeg? *What if* we'd taken them in Ralph's BMW with proper wheels and all the air bags you'd ever need? *What if* we'd sent them off three hours earlier? *What if* Brittany had only flown out Monday and not rushed back. *What if* ... Oh, if only I hadn't taken them to Mexico, if only we'd ....

I realized at the time, this was beyond us. We really had no control. The *if only* would go back all the way to, "IF only they had not been born, this would not have happened." We would drive ourselves even further around the bend if we followed that route, of all the unchangeable and taunting *what if's and if onlys*. No blame for each other; we could not undo this event ...

Oh, but *if only we could go back in time.*

After all this trauma we had to drive forty-five minutes across the city to another hospital where Brittany had been taken. The accident victims had been routed to two different hospitals to deal with the emergency.

Again, we were escorted, this time along a long dark corridor. It was as though I could see us from above, my heart aching for these people who were going into *that room* of incomprehensible grief. Curt and Deb waited outside the room. Alone in the room was my beautiful, precious baby, nineteen years old ... such a beautiful girl ... just a few hours ago so full of life and spunk ... now lifeless.

I looked at her and imagined I saw her chest rise ... I went up to her and put my head on her chest ... "Breathe Britt, come on, breathe." ... I cannot accept two dead children in one night. Lord this is too much......... "Oh Breathe, Brittany Jane Marie, BREATHE!!"

As if my will could put life and breath back into her body. But God, you can do it; please, she cannot be dead. Dead is too final.

No, God. No, God. Please, No God.

Curtis and Debbie drove us home that night. They drove our car and we sat in the back seat ... unable to comprehend what had just happened. There is nothing to say when faced with a tragedy of this magnitude.

The next few days continued in a state of shock. As the first florist arrived at the door, I said to my sister, "I don't want any damn flowers." I knew once flowers arrived, it was real; flowers verified the tragedy. I wanted to pretend it hadn't happened, it couldn't have happened ... "Someone please wake me up!"

People had heard. Bad news travels quickly, and horrible news hits other people before you can even acknowledge it yourself. Often people do not know what to do in such a situation of tragedy, so they send flowers to let people know, "You are in our thoughts and prayers." But I didn't want to have to be in people's thoughts and prayers. *I wanted* to send flowers. *I wanted* to pray for other people....

Lord I don't want this.

From my journal:

*** *Tuesday, March 1, 2005*

Waves of pain & crying come over me.

Yesterday, actually from Sun 6:45 pm the next 24 hours have been the longest day in my life. But Lord there will be more long days ahead.

Joan shared with me that God is saving each of our tear drops—He is collecting them.

He is aware of each one and He is sharing in them. ***

It felt as if I had cried an ocean of tears already; And I believed that *Jesus wept*

The flowers kept coming....... They wept with us and over-
flowed the living room to the funeral home, they flooded with
sympathy....... the earth wept in flowers.

I am blessed with good family support. I had sisters take
over answering the phone, receiving messages, and giving
me water to drink, to replenish the tears.

We tried to get through to our daughter, Kristen. The most
horrible phone call to make, is to tell your oldest child that
she has just lost both her siblings. Not even sure what day or
time it was, probably somewhere on Monday ... thankfully,
Mildred, my son-in-law's mother, initiated the phone calls to
start the process to bring Kristen and Kevin back to Canada.
She had contacted their team leader, Dave, who traveled
two hours to tell Kristen that she needed to call her parents
in Canada.

The phone rang. I took the call in the computer room.
Kristen was on the line calling from the island of Zanzibar,
Tanzania, as they'd had a few days reprieve from their village
life, but it was hard for her to hear with the poor connection.

"Kristen... Jordan and Brittany were in an accident."
Silence ... as if she was afraid to ask anything. This is *the
dreaded call* that people never, ever want to get. There was no
way to soften the blow and with the intermittent connection I
just had to say, "They were killed." She did not seem to hear
or understand ... I had to shout it in the phone.... "Jordan and
Brittany are dead; they are both dead." I heard the phone drop,
cries of pain, I wanted to somehow reach through the phone
and wrap my arms around her. I wanted to keep this from
happening. But I was powerless to do anything but inform
her of the nightmare that had just arrived at her doorstep.

I heard Kevin asking her, "What?" S*ilence.* Kevin picked
up the phone and I continued the conversation with him.
Fortunately, their team leader was with them. Dave had

already begun the arrangements for sending them home to Canada......

The next days of planning a funeral moved in a dream-like state. We knew we needed to honour the amazing lives Jordan and Brittany had managed to live in such a few short years. Of course, in our eyes they were exceptional young people, and as the encouraging stories began to pour in, we were made aware that many other people thought that as well.

People came in and out of the house, always people present. Food and flowers delivered nonstop.

Sometimes I did not know where to leave myself, what to do.

Oh Lord, I want to be someone else. But it felt as if I was. It was as if I was watching from the outside and thinking, *who is this poor woman? How could anyone cope with such a tragedy?*

And then the continuous decision making that assaulted our shock. When to have the funeral? What food do you want? What about special music? Do you want pictures put up? Who should speak? Do you want a reserved section for work colleagues? My work colleagues? This is my children's funeral? A funeral I do not want. There may be reporters from the Winnipeg Free Press, are you ok with that?

In a heartbroken daze my husband and I, along with my sister Vicki and brother-in-law Ray went to select coffins. No one should have to select a coffin for a child, and now we had to select two. The undertaker requested we provide clothing for our son and daughter to wear, including underwear. It was surreal. What a strange thing; I had not dressed my children since they were kids, what would they want to wear? I remembered Ralph comments on Britt's casual dress style "If she wanted to dress like a laundry hamper, she should wait till she had the face and body to go with it." She never

9

realized her great beauty, and had not been caught up with the latest of fashion. My mind went back to the time of her high school graduation, less than two years earlier; she wore a stunning orange gown. It was $300, by no means out of line with the price of the day, but I had wondered about spending that amount of money on a dress for one night. Now as I realized, I would never get to have the joy of shopping for her wedding dress, I was glad I had purchased the grad gown of her choice. But that certainly was not going to be the dress to wear in the coffin. What does one wear in the coffin? Oh the questions that kept coming.

Jordan and Brittany's funeral was on March 5, 2005. My father's funeral had been March 5, 1991. It had been fourteen years earlier to the day. My mother said to me, "Finally, Dad has someone else in heaven with him." I did not appreciate the comment and told her it would've been fine if someone else had gone to keep him company. My father did not need my two children to keep him company in Heaven. He'd been there for fourteen years; I'm sure he would have made his own connections. Later in time, I did wonder if my father and Jordan ever played guitar together.

The scriptures chosen for the funeral were from Lamentations and Psalm 62, NIV.

Arise, cry out in the night, as the watches of the night begin;
pour out your heart like water in the presence of the Lord.
Lift up your hands to Him for the lives of your children.
Lam 2:19,20
I well remember them and my soul is downcast within me,
Yet this I call to mind and therefore I have hope:
Because of the Lord's great love we are not consumed
for His compassions never fail.

They are new every morning; great is your faithfulness.
Lam 3:19-23
Though he brings grief, he will show compassion,
so great is his unfailing love,
For he does not willingly bring affliction or grief to the children of men. Lam 3:32,33

I had to believe these verses were true. I had to believe that He did not willingly bring grief to us.

Did that make sense? At this time, it felt as though nothing made any sense.

The only thing that was real, was incredible pain and emptiness.

The sun shone that day, when rain would have been more fitting. The woman I saw dressed in black turned out to be me. She knelt, a six foot hole on either side of her. "We do not grieve as those without hope," she whispered with determined conviction, as she said good by to her precious treasures. Would that hope carry her?

The day after the funeral is the worst day of your life. It is even worse than the funeral day, because, there is a hollowness and a knowing that it will get much darker before it gets any better.

The following weeks were a blur of trying to participate in life, but having zero energy to do it. I was going through the motions, and yet, as I struggled with many things ... God was there ... and as my spirit asked many unanswered questions, He was there, providing strength to cope with the moment, at times a sense of peace; quite honestly, it was probably shock.

Once you have two deposits in heaven you start to wonder about things ... especially the reality of life after death. I had always believed in life after death. It was comforting to be reassured by the preacher at your grandparent's funeral that these wonderful old souls, who had already lived a good life, would be up there with God, sitting on a cloud playing a harp. I had never really given it that much thought. Even when my father died, which brought it much closer to home, I did not doubt that he was with God, smiling down on us, perhaps playing guitar with Johnny Cash.

But now—this was the Mount Everest of doubts. I was asking God to use my little seed of faith to say to that mountain *Jump* and it should. Wasn't that the scripture?

I had taken some classes, where it was all theoretical, on pre- and post-millennial judgement, resurrection, discussions back in the lofty days of Bible College. But that was all theory. This was life and death, even more critical, it was *my* children's life and death and it took my breath away.

Two conflicting concepts that arose out of the scriptures for me were: first—"This day you will be with me in paradise." Second—"The trumpet shall sound, the dead in Christ will rise first and meet Him in the air, and so we will all be with the Lord Jesus." There are more references about those who are "asleep in the Lord."

As if they would be awakened with the trumpet alarm clock.

My big concern was that Jordan, Brittany and Jamie were just in *nether-land* until the cows would come home or some trumpet would give a final blast. That was such a devastating blow to me. I wanted to *know* that they were with God, and with Him from the moment their spirits left their bodies on the curve on that icy road. *I NEEDED to know*. I spoke to a few people, including the pastors. Pastors fear hurting people in sorrow and somehow their lack of conviction only increased my angst over the whole scenario. I do not know why it was such a big issue for me, but it was.

And this was where the spirit prompted my brother Curtis with answers for me.

From my journal, not dated but somewhere in the first week:

*** *Remember the words of Curt:*

> *"God is not under the restraints of time.*
> *He creates and rules over it.*
> *(God's) Time is not on the same dimension.*
> *We have a straight-forward time line.*
> *God can move forward & backwards & sideways."*

So yes they can be immediately in Your arms, & when the trumpet calls the dead in Christ will rise & it all works because You are NOT RESTRAINED BY TIME.

Praise the Lord. I NEEDED TO KNOW THIS. ***

When discussing eternity, I used to joke "Heaven is forever, anyways. I'm in no hurry to get there. Apparently, we will have until the end of time to enjoy it .... What is the rush?"

In an instant, any fear of death was gone. In fact, there were days I would much have preferred death to life. Ralph and I wondered aloud about things .... understanding why people choose to end their lives. We spoke those things to each other. The heaviness and the weight of the question of meaning and purpose in this life was upon us. We felt we were suffocating. Scripturally, death is the result of *Adam's sin* .... and we were now experiencing the overpowering grief it bore.

"God, did you struggle so much to lose your son?"

I knew I would never *give up my son for anyone's sake*, as God had done. And yet my head argued, it was easier for God to do it, in fact I thought it was, all fine and dandy. God knew that Jesus would be with him again soon. We live with such uncertainty; we don't have that same infinite outlook. But what had I been taught and what did I believe? And what did the Bible actually say? We are *human* after all!!

This uncertainty compelled me to read all sorts of books.

You know you are in trouble when your book titles read: *Just enough Light for the Step I'm on, How to Survive the Loss of a Loved One, Heaven, Dancing in the Dark,* A *Grace Disguised, Where is God when it Hurts? Disappointment with God.*

There were books on grief that I read part way, some I finished. If it was not helpful, I abandoned it and went on to a different one. Looking, seeking, and hoping for some words of comfort that could begin to anesthetize the pain of my soul.

I read ravenously, wanting to numb the pain, find a hope or promise of relief. I needed concrete evidence. In fact, it would have been the best to have a personal visit with God or His son.

The psalms became important and yet they caused a lot of struggle. In them I found numerous promises, that seemed to be unfulfilled. My heart cried out, "Why do you say you will never leave me or forsake me when I feel so alone and forsaken, God?"

Yes, the imagery of footprints in the sand came to mind. Surprisingly we'd only been given about four copies of that poem, either in a card or plaque, but I understood as well, when the writer was being carried in the sand ... he still felt as if he was struggling alone. "Will it only be when I look back that I can see you were always there?" I wanted to know and feel His presence *now*, not just in the future that He had been with me.

From my journal, a poem written for us by cousin, Abe Hildebrand:

*** *Tinker Creek Reflections*
A shroud of white blankets a
barren and lifeless tree.
The Sun appears and droplets of water glisten
at the ragged edge of crusted snow.
A Heart is wrapped in cold white grief.
We ask the Son to come and gently unwrap
the icy shroud of pain. ***

Once tragedy struck, there was no escape. I could not get out of it. Shock was a blessed thing ... it numbed my mind and soul all too briefly, as the searing pain of the dark hole had me in fetal position. I do believe that it was the shock that gave me the out of body sensation; making me feel as if I was looking at my life and experiencing it from the outside, watching this poor lady deal with the overwhelming task of coming to terms with the loss of two children.

Shock lets you go through the motions; it lets people walk on broken legs. Initially they do not recognize what has happened; they try to behave in a normal fashion. "What is normal???" Oh I longed for something normal, but it was gone, along with hopes and dreams of a future. It became a struggle to cope with more than ten minutes at a time.

I felt so utterly alone ... Grief is a very, very lonely journey.

CHAPTER TWO

WALKING

Walk on, walk on
The road gets so lonely the shoes get kind of thin
I don't know where I'm going, but I sure know where
I've been
Walk on, walk on
You got to keep on walking till you find your way.
    Brownie McGhee/ sung by Ruthie Foster

And so I walked, and walked.

We had a footpath in the park across the road from our house, and I walked, preferably early in the morning or late at night in the darkness, so I would not meet people.

The act of walking is a simple process of putting one foot in front of the other. As I walked, I could talk with God. The song I would sing or say as I started my walk was:

"God you are my God, I want to ever praise you.

Let me seek you in the morning, let me learn to walk in your ways

and step by step please lead me, I want to follow you all of my days"

I would need to add, *"And that includes TODAY."*

Our tragedy hit the front pages of the Winnipeg Free Press, one of the *heart stories* about these great young adults, who had come back from spending two weeks working at an orphanage in Mexico and were tragically killed. There were ten deaths on the roads that weekend in our province, an all-time-high due to the dangerous ice conditions. It was one day in the news, a 'sad read' for everyone else, and a lifetime for those involved in the story.

People overwhelmed us with support, but nothing could ease the sorrow.

CLEANING JORDAN'S APARTMENT

From my journal:

*** Teach me how to know death
and go on with life.
Teach me how to love life
and not fear death.

Judith Viorst

Sat March 12—I think. Tomorrow will be 2 weeks since the accident. 2 weeks ago we were flying home from Mexico. I remember thinking I didn't want to just get back into 'the rat race.' Well I'm not. Now I don't know what 'normal' is and shallow ordinary would be ok.

We're on our way to Winnipeg to check out Jord's apt. Bring his things home—I want to just leave it there—hoping he might come back, wishing this all were not so—how strange ... everything is so unreal.

When I quote the grieving book it's, Grieving the Loss of Someone You Love by Raymond Mitsch and Lynn Brookside. It's excellent, we've been reading it aloud.

"Those who live the abundant life seem to seize each experience, tragic or joyous and squeeze every drop of learning out of it into their cup of life. Some of us are envious of their .... quality of lifestyle, but we have forgotten what price that kind of honesty and courage has cost."

Joyce Landorf, quoted in the above grieving book.

5:30 pm We're on our way home. It hurts to see how much Ralph is hurting today. It just doesn't make any sense to him. He says he feels like he might be in the angry stage. Jord, Jamie & Britt had so much to offer the Lord in their service for Him. Lord protect his heart. He wants to be more faithful and Ralph has made some phenomenal changes already. He looks so sad, it hurts so bad.

We cleaned up Jord's apt. This was a place he just loved — or this part of his life, he seemed to be so happy here. So many painful reminders of a young man in love, snuffed out at the start of life. ***

The most powerful image from the apartment was a painting our son had been working on, it was set on an easel as we entered his bedroom and I dubbed it, *"An Unfinished Life"*. Other poignant reminders, pictures of Jamie—the love of his life, hand written notes from her, financial records, cookbooks—he'd gotten into cooking, everything cried out for someone to return to this place and finish the unfinished life.

From there we went to see the place where Jordan had been employed for a few months, the dining area of a senior's complex. The elderly clients apparently loved him there, many people wrote notes to us, filled with words of appreciation for Jordan's kindness, his warm smile and caring ways. It was good to know he'd been appreciated and would be missed, but I knew others would easily take his place in the work situation, but who or what would take his place in our lives?? The emptiness loomed so large it was about to swallow us whole.

From my journal:

*** *Wed. March 16—Day 17 of a life I don't want to live.*

> *"Your love is the shelter over my soul*
> *You will hear the humble and the broken*
> **Mercy falls like a river running wild."** *(Lines*
> *from a song)*

Please Lord, send your love and mercy.

Found out yesterday—Britt's password to get into her hotmail account was "jesuschrist".

Lord that moved me to tears. You were her password to life. Lord I am so humbled by her dedication to you. Lord grant me the growth to live up to my daughter's witness.

Jesus Christ, please help me. Today is not so bad—but it just feels HOLLOW.

If I repeat myself, it is No wonder—I hardly know who I am.

"Who is living this life??" "Who is talking out of my mouth?? Who is living this horrible life??" These are the questions we keep asking ourselves. I know people cannot understand. I didn't know before this either.

Book title I saw at the Blessings Book store, Dear God, I Liked My Life Before, When it was Superficial............ I'd woken up feeling deep despair, a bit later I looked out the window and saw neighborhood kids going to school. All of a sudden, I realized—of course, it's a school day. Everyone's life is NORMAL— mine is not. What kind of normal will there ever be for us?

Katie B phoned and asked what she could pray for—I said against despair.

Kris D came over with a French Vanilla cappuccino from Tim's—that was good.

I realize I need the support of people around me—Lord, we do not want Satan to defeat us with hopelessness and despair—Please give us a glimmer of hope.

3 pm same day—feels like it's a Long day. Herb (pastor) just came over, he asked "What was a good thing about today?" My response, "that no one could hear me as I wailed in the shower." I had a meltdown there in the shower—wasn't even crying so much as wailing—not even sure if they were real tears or they were just washed away by the water pouring over me. I phoned Mom to see if she could come over to help me. The book says we don't even want to admit to people that we can't do the 'usual' household chores. I phoned Mom to help me do the laundry and clean my bathroom. I realize life is even more chaotic when the house is a mess.

I'm eating some comfort foods—plain potato chips & coke.

It's sunny out & I think I'll go for another walk. ***

From my journal:

*** Herb prayed for us and told us we were doing well—NO WE'RE Not, we're doing LOUSY & I WANT MY OLD LIFE BACK!!

All the pictures around, family pics of the kids, etc., will they be too painful?? Right now I want everyone to know how great our kids were. Oh that hurts to write past tense, were.

How ironic

I've always prayed for God's best in our children's lives and now they've actually got His best, Heaven ... I'D LIKE TO TAKE IT BACK.

Think I'll go for another walk.

Lord, Keep holding us. Some days it's hard to breathe. ***

At the end of each day, lying side by side, Ralph and I would look heavenward and say, "Good night Jord. Good night Britt. Love you," and then drift into the corners of our minds. If aided by medication, we might drift into sleep, if not, it would be a rehashing of thoughts and events.

PILGRIMAGE TO BANFF

Before Kristen and Kevin went back to Africa, we travelled together as a family—the remaining four of us, to Canmore, Alberta to pick up our youngest daughter's belongings. What a change. Just four months earlier I'd gone to visit her, still brimming with excitement for this new start in her life. With the enthusiasm of a nineteen-year-old eager to take on the world, she had driven the seventeen hours to Banff in her small maroon Chevy Cavalier to kick off this life of independence. While Ralph and I were in Kenya that September of 2004, visiting Kristen and Kevin, we received the email that Brittany had arrived safely in Banff. She'd boldly picked up a hitch-hiker en route, found a place for him for the night while she stayed with friends in Briercrest. The next day they continued on the journey, and she shared the gospel with him, as they passed the miles. Brittany was our *missionary in dread-locks*, as her friends affectionately called her, her love of life and adventure evident in all she did. How could she possibly be gone, oh Lord? The church where she'd been attending for a few months had held a memorial service for her, and a week later members of the congregation gathered around to pray for us when we paid a visit. In her short time in Banff, she had made a difference. Pastor Norm of the Banff Park Church shared verses on grief and comfort, I believe largely because he knew we were coming. It also was evident that this church had been impacted by our daughter's life and her untimely death.

From my journal:

*** *Banff Park Church*

We had an awesome evening. Pastor Norm gave an excellent talk about grief & comfort—"God is our comfort. He is all we need. Some of our suffering happens so we do not rely on ourselves, but on God." They called us up and surrounded us, different people prayed for us. I appreciated one lady who prayed for our marriage to endure this and that we would become stronger. ***

Total strangers, yet powerfully connected by suffering and the hope we share! The request that struck a chord with me was that of the lady who clearly and fervently interceded for our marriage. The thought crossed my mind that although I knew statistics were bad for a marriage to survive the loss of a child, surely, Lord, that would not be our situation—we had endured enough.

The highlight of that trip, if there can be a highlight on a trip of that nature, was picking up a commemorative rock, from the banks of the Bow River. For my birthday just five weeks earlier, Britt had given me a picture of her and her friends, posed with a couch along this riverbank. A very artsy shot, done in a hand crafted frame she had put together of wood twigs. The picture and her tales of how she and three friends borrowed a truck, hauled this pink couch to the riverbank and then took photos, had us laughing at the whole escapade. A professional photographer had come upon the scene as they were in the midst of their crazy antics, and offered to take a few shots for them.

In honour of Britt, and the connection that she and I had for rock collecting, it was decided a rock from the Bow River would need to be taken for my rose garden. On numerous previous trips my youngest daughter and I collected rocks, stopping the vehicle in different places to pilfer stones from the roadside and then haul them home to the garden. Memories of us tramping through the snow along the shores of Lake Louise, on a recent ski trip flooded my mind. We had searched for the perfect rock to sneak back with us, nearly slipped into open water to get *The Rock*, then took turns hiding it under our ski jackets, as we shoplifted it past the official naturalists and park people. We presumed they would not have shared our enthusiasm for the stone removal. Now in true incognito style, Kristen and I selected a fairly large rock with great colourings, covered it with a black plastic garbage bag and then tried to lift it. Using good body techniques, we squatted down and on the count of three lifted, carried it about ten steps, and then had to let it down either due to our laughter, or the fact that it was too heavy to carry any further. From the truck tailgate, we could hear Ralph and Kevin as they laughed uproariously at our stumbling efforts to bring the rock up. Did they stop and help us out? No, they continued to munch Dorito chips and howl. It was a great moment; in spite of everything, we laughed and laughed, even more than the situation warranted, allowing the laughter to relieve some of the stress. There had not been many occasions for hilarity and we relished it.

On the return to Manitoba, we ran into snowy weather and poor road conditions in Regina. With the experience of years of ski trips, we knew Regina historically to be a bad spot. We were compelled to stop for the night.

There was not a lot to do. Ralph was engaged in reading the book, *Heaven* by Randy Alcorn. I felt the need to get out and walk, so I left the room to see what lay beyond our hotel. There was a little book-store in the vicinity and I soon found myself in that shop. Due to the inclement weather, there were few customers and within five minutes, I was alone in the store with the clerk.

Over the store sound system, I heard the beginning of a song ... then I recognized it. I nearly buckled over in disbelief ... "God is this some kind of cruel joke?" Silence except for the music. "How dare you mock me with this song?" All the energy sapped out from me. I stood motionless waiting for the words to come; pain tore at my soul as Leanne Womack sang:

"When you get the choice to sit it out or dance /I hope you dance. Don't let some hell-bent heart leave you bitter/ when you're close to giving up reconsider/ give the heavens above more than a passing glance ... and when you get the choice to sit it out or dance/ DANCE."

"God, if you want me to dance again, I will need some serious healing going on."

Was it just seven weeks ago that I had stood boldly before my birthday crowd and told them that I wanted to live whole-heartedly for God? For years I had lived with a cautious optimism, holding back as though I was expecting some great disaster, never fully trusting God. And yet He had always been there for me, had taken me through life's ups and downs and I wanted to move beyond the compromised trust and passion. I wanted to dance with life and with God. This was the very song that I featured for my 50th birthday dance. In this little bookshop I wanted to curl up and die in agony as my words came back to taunt me. I felt betrayed by God. Was there a possibility I would *ever* want to dance again?

The next day, on the final miles of our journey back to Winkler, Ralph became anxious about getting back before the snow made driving conditions worse. He started to speed up and I remember feeling a sense of concern as he accelerated along the road. Kristen and I suggested that he slow down, but it seemed his foot would become heavy again. Suddenly the red and blue police lights were flashing in our rear-view mirror. This was a 100 kilometer per hour zone and we were probably doing 118. Ralph pulled over. As the officer stood at the window, he asked if we could explain why we were traveling so fast. "Can you give me any reason that I should not give you a ticket?"

Ralph muttered something about compassion, and wanting to get home before it was too icy. The officer suggested we would do better to slow down. As he prepared to write the ticket, I said "Why don't you tell him what's really happened?"

Ralph said, "No," but I turned to the officer, "Excuse me, we just lost two children on icy roads and have now come back from Banff to pick up our deceased daughters belongings. Yes, we know we were speeding, and sir, we are just not quite ourselves."

He stopped in his tracks, then thoughtfully suggested we should, "Slow down to live," and walked away from the car. This shook all of us up.

Back in Winkler, we began the most difficult task of trying to fit back into normal life. Nothing seemed normal.

As the days sped by for other people, all that we had known had changed so very suddenly. It was difficult to find meaning in life and a reason to get up in the morning. Ralph went back to work to give his mind something else to think about. In the next weeks, I could see more and more heaviness descend on Ralph's heart and soul. The journey of grief is lonely. I wished for some way to lighten the load for him. I read voraciously, listened to music and walked. Most every day someone would come by to try to encourage me or both of us. Mercifully, time started to move back into some semblance of rhythm.

"Time is too slow for those who wait, too swift for those who fear, too long for those who grieve, too short for those who rejoice, but for those who love, Time is Eternity."

Henry Van Dyke

CHAPTER THREE

MINIMAL SPRING

We faced many momentous events in the first few weeks. That first Easter was a struggle. It had been three weeks since the funeral and I had not been out in public much. Kristen wondered if I really wanted to go to church, but I said, "Yes." I thought it should be good, especially since we were celebrating the resurrection. Of all things I needed to be assured of, it was the reality of the resurrection. So we went to church, went to our usual pew near the front left hand side of the sanctuary. People gave us smiles, pats on the back, mini hugs as we came by. Very quickly I realized that this was more difficult than I had thought it would be. When we stood up to sing, "Death where is thy victory, grave where is thy sting," my inner being revolted. The sting of death was very fresh, real and evident. It felt as though I had been punched in the stomach and could not get my breath.

People wanted to talk to Kristen and Kevin after church, as they had been away for over a year. I simply could not face people. As I passed a group of my friends, I could sense the conversation slow down as I neared. They were talking about normal things, which seemed so frivolous to me at the time. I felt like an outsider. I went to the car, trying to avoid the looks of passersby, waiting for the others to come. By the time they returned I was in tears and my daughter felt badly for having made me wait. The energy was drained from me. I told them they should go to Ralph's family for the Easter dinner. There was no way I could handle it in my state.

There was an outpouring of support for us, and prior to the funeral, we had decided that in lieu of flowers, monies could be designated for the Winkler Bible Camp (WBC), for a project to be determined later. Jordan and Brittany, as well as our eldest daughter, had spent many summers at the camp. Initially they had attended with a short stint as campers, but later spent much more time as camp staff. A few summers we had thought that Jordan or Brittany should have been making real money to go to school; but each season they spent as staff at WBC solidified their walk in faith, and the direction they were setting for their futures. People shared stories that encouraged us as parents, of what an impact these two had had on the lives of many others. The donations flowed in, causing us to realize a *big* project would need to be decided upon. As Kristen and Kevin had also spent time there, we wanted their input in the decision-making process. In a small meeting with some of the camp administration, an idea was born. Ralph and I were thinking small; Kristen had some grand ideas. "Jordan always thought it would be great if the camp had a lake."

That was a *wow* project that would gather momentum as time progressed.

Kristen and Kevin (K&K) remained in Canada for about six weeks, leaving in early April to resume their studies in Kenya. That too was a difficult departure, but we realized that our daughter should, and probably would, have a better chance of moving on to a good life and possibly be less affected by the tragedy than her parents were. It was still more than one should bear at her young age; she was only twenty-five, and seemed to have experienced more suffering than many people twice her age; first, through their time in Kenya with life threatening illness, and now this tragedy. We wondered if this was all part of the enemy's desire to defeat them in their life's work? Was the enemy waging war? When passionate young people like Jamie, Jordan and Brittany, are taken from life early, many questions arise. In our own ways, we all tried to come up with an understanding of the situation. Maybe we would not get an answer on this side of heaven.

As I looked for greater meaning and purpose in all of this, the clichés seemed to defy logic and became more hollow. Death was just so *final*, so *difficult*, so *senseless*, seemingly so *random*. The only thing we knew for sure was that it carried with it such despair and anguish, that we wondered if we could survive.

I read one book on grieving, where a Christian lady apparently never shed a tear for her daughter's death, stoically believing this was what God allowed and wanted, and so kept her grief to herself. Well, I shed so many tears I thought the well would run dry, but there was always a new occasion to open the floodgates.

April also signalled the beginning of spring. In the past it had always been a sign of new life and hope; a season to look forward to. As an avid gardener spring had always been my favorite time of the year, with its freshness, the newness of life, and the beauty of it bursting out from the frozen landscape. This year the cloud of death overshadowed everything.

The endless arguments and debates going on in my head were relentless.

All that I had believed in, everything I had based my life on was questioned.

Could I trust this God I had believed in my whole life?

What was the meaning of all this?

Was there any meaning, any purpose whatsoever?
Had I passed on the truth to my children??
Was there any Truth?

BIRTHDAYS

Both Jordan and Brittany were born in April, on the tenth and twenty-ninth respectively. What to do, how do you celebrate a birthday, when people are dead and should not be? They should be alive, so *alive* ... and they were not ... their bodies were six feet under in a cold place.

On April 10, the florist delivered a beautiful bouquet of white roses, twenty-two of them: the number to match the age Jordan should have been. On the 29th of April, the same florist delivered twenty exquisite pink roses. They were ordered ahead of time by our daughter, who was now back in Kenya.

To commemorate both their birthdays, we had some of their friends come over for supper. We served loaded nachos with Ralph's famous homemade salsa and ordered the kids favorite pizza. We sat around, talking, laughing, and sharing memories. Between supper and dessert, our small group went to the cemetery and released twenty-eight helium balloons on which we had written messages. We released them for Jordan and Brittany. Symbolically, it was a great thing to do. After that, we returned home for a family favourite dessert: chocolate chip cheesecake.

From my journal:

*** *Sun April 10, 2005 Jordan's 22nd birthday and we got to bring birthday cake to the cemetery—How special is that??! Lord I pray against bitterness, against envy and despair. Last night we had BBQ steak, & ate outside, for his birthday. Then went to the cemetery. Don & Karen stopped by with a* *strawberry torte—how thoughtful of her. Curtis phoned to say they were remembering us, as did many others. Last night about 10:40 pm I was getting ready for bed and I heard a knock at the door. Al & Irene came by to say bedtime prayers with us. Al was in his pyjamas and so was I. Thank you Lord, for how your people show their care and your love. At the cemetery I noted other people had also left flowers and notes.*

So today—Jord's birthday, we called K&K, they were en route to the village. The phone did not work well; we struggled with connections, after 5 or 6 times it seemed to be ok. Oh yes did I mention I got my period a week early? I laughed out loud when I checked my supplies, cuz Kristen had put a little encouragement note in the supplies box ... Lord I am a high needs person right now. Emotionally I am barely hanging in there. ***

Spring came a little earlier that year, and I noted in my journal, that perhaps Britt had asked God to go kindly on us and bless us with a warm spring. By the end of April, I had ten different flowers blooming. I cried as the tulips came up that year, recalling the time when Britt was sixteen. Some of her friends had come over to say *hi* while I'd been working in the back yard. It was a warm day and as I went to the spot where the tulips first come up, I could see the red-green tips of the plants just poking through the soil. It always excited me to see them ... I ran around to the front to share this marvellous revelation with Britt, unaware that she had friends there. All the girls came back to view the tulips. The girls expected real flowers, but Britt had the gardener's heart and shared the joy with me as we viewed the little beginnings poking through.

One of the things mentioned in the grieving book is that you might think you see your child again. This totally caught me off guard when it happened. I was walking along a pathway and a young man in a brown plaid shirt rode a bicycle onto the path ahead of me and my mind said, "That's Jordan." This young man's bike riding gait was so similar to my son's loping style, I quickened my pace to get a better look as he disappeared out of sight. I wanted to run after him, hold him, ask him to stay ... but instead I went home and broke down in sobs. I realized I would never again have that chance. The effects of shock were wearing off, the emotional nerve endings were beginning to feel, the darkness and pain were severe. My heart was an open wound.

After Kristen and Kevin returned to Kenya, I went back to work, but found it difficult to focus. I had always loved my work in the operating room as a scrub/circulating nurse. It was enjoyable talking to patients, easing their pre-surgical nervousness with lighthearted or serious discussion, depending on their need. Now I found it a challenge to learn anything new or to be motivated about new surgical techniques. I had minimal interest in the latest knee replacement. I dreaded going to work. On more than one early morning drive to the hospital, I had to stave off the tears. Previously my ten minute ride had been used as a time to pray for my children and now, as my mind would automatically begin the blessing for Kristen, Jordan and Brittany, I ached and wondered what I would pray for. Kristen and Kevin were in need of increased intercession, but this was one more jab to the heart. One of my daughter's friends had wondered who would pray for her now, as Brittany had been her faithful prayer warrior.

Isaiah 41:13 NIV carried me through many a day. *"For I am the Lord, your God, who takes hold of your right hand and says to you, Do not fear, I will help you."* I pleaded that verse. I lifted my right hand as I walked and demanded that God do that, take my hand and walk with me, remove my fear.

Part of the difficulty was that we were so well known in our community. Ralph had a business that employed about 150 people in our town. We were involved in our church; people were aware of our situation and often did not know what to say to us. After initial conversations of encouragement, there seemed little to say. It was difficult to ask them how their kids were doing; it reminded us of our great loss. Many of our friends and work colleagues had children the same ages as ours and their lives continued while ours had stopped dead in its tracks. But work brought with it some sense of structure and a forced opportunity to focus on things other than grief. It became easier to connect with people in pain.

I remember a day that a young mother of two came in for a central line insertion—that on its own is not a good sign. Usually these lines are inserted either for chemotherapy or for some type of long term antibiotic medication. This lady had been diagnosed with Hodgkins during her recent pregnancy. She had a toddler and a newborn, and had needed to wait until her child was born to begin the chemo treatment. Hodgkins is usually treatable if caught early. She told me how on the night before, her older child had needed a lot of attention, probably sensing something was not right with his mommy. He kept coming to her to say, "Kiss it better, Mommy, kiss it better." So she would kiss him and he would be content for a while. This scenario was repeated several times. She finally told him he needed to go to bed, because Mommy had to go to bed, so she wouldn't get sick. The little boy left and then came back one final time with, "Kiss it better on the inside, Mommy."

Oh Lord, I nearly broke down and cried ... "Yes. Kiss us better on the inside."

Out of the mouths of babes.

And the look, the look of utter pity as people would recognize me in the store and avoid glancing in my direction, or

I in theirs. I decided to stay away from public places for the sake of other people as well as my own. Ralph and I seemed to bring with us a great discomfort; many people were ill at ease in our presence.

But the concept of walking is about putting one foot in front of the other. Walking only requires that you take one step at a time. And that was all we could handle.

The first wedding we went to was a complete disaster for me. We should not have gone, but we felt the pressure, because it was a niece. The pastor made some joke about the groom's choice of passage, Psalm 57. The groom had actually chosen Psalm 67. The joke went on and on about the day of disaster that was referred to in the incorrect passage, that the groom had not chosen. Did the pastor not know this family had recently experienced an actual day of disaster? I felt it was extremely insensitive. Ralph and I struggled to make it through the ceremony, deciding to forgo the reception. By the time I left I was so upset, I wailed the entire drive home. All night long, in my head I was arguing with the pastor, on how stupid and insensitive I thought his joke had been. This experience left my confidence shattered for trying to be out in public. Another wedding guest called me the next day to express her concern and her recognition that the wedding ceremony had probably been extremely difficult for us.

From my journal:

*** Oh Lord, I felt so cheated. We were supposed to be able to begin planning Jordan & Jamie's wedding and instead we had over 2,000 people come to their funerals ... Hold me up Lord. I don't know how much more of this I can take. ***

CHAPTER FOUR

WHAT DREAMS MAY COME

There seems to be a phenomenon of supernatural dreams or experiences that may occur following the death of a loved one. This was mentioned in several of the books I'd read, and also spoken of by people who had experienced this. Unwittingly Ralph and I became members of a club we never wanted to join, the entry fee was much too steep, the exclusive 'community club' of people who have lost a child, or children, as in our case. As a result of speaking with others who'd experienced these dreams, we began to wonder about and to long for a dream in which our kids would be present. Apparently, the more common experience indicated that it would happen sooner rather than later. It was almost as if we anticipated this event happening. For some reason, I asked God if only one of us could have a dream, that it would come to Ralph, as he seemed even more in need of a sign than I did.

Psalm 116:15 NIV *"Precious in the sight of the Lord is the death of His saints."*

The evening of February 27, Jamie's mother sensed the presence of angels in the hospital rooms where Jamie and Jordan were. I had no reason to doubt her. It brought comfort to know that Heaven took notice of this event.

FIRST

Our first experience with a dream came via an older gentleman from our church family. Norm was one of the well-loved seniors in church, white haired, sparkling blue-green eyes, with the kind of genuine smile that warms the heart. He always took a special interest in the young people, making a point to engage them in conversation whenever he had the chance, or asking their parents how they were doing. More than once he told me how he had first gotten to know our son Jordan, at a Youth meet the Seniors event. Norm had walked into the church dining hall, feeling a bit out of place, even though this was arranged for the seniors to attend. The round tables had been set up with crokinole (Knipspratt) game boards. Hesitantly he waited, but it was only a few minutes before a smiling Jordan had come up to him, engaged him in conversation and asked him to become partners in the foursome game. Our kids felt a special connection with Norm, so it was interesting and a blessing to have him talk to us of a vision, a dream he had been given.

When we read the card with Norm's vision, we were on our pilgrimage to Canmore to pick up Brittany's belongings. There were so many cards from the funeral that we had not had time to read them, and now I came upon Norm's.

From my journal:

*** *Friday March 18, 2005*

Psalm 84:10. Just heard the song line, "Better is one day in your house, better is one day in your courts, than thousands elsewhere."

I guess Jordan, Britt and Jamie are in your courts. Praise you for that.

We read more sympathy cards en route yesterday. Wow—thank you Lord for Norm Groening and the vision he had. He shared about he & his wife going to the funeral home and him being overcome with our incomprehensible loss. Then they went home and he told me, while he was praying he got a vivid picture of Jesus sitting with Jordan on his right, with Jesus' arm kind of around and behind him, and Jamie also there on Jesus' left arm. Brittany was in front of Him with her arms outstretched to Him. Norm said he did not usually get visions, but felt he needed to share this with us for comfort. PTL! Thank you Jesus. Ralph & I had tears in our eyes as I read this. We were both looking for a sign also. ***

SECOND

Another unusual dream event involved a friend from Australia that Brittany had gotten to know while she was in Canmore. Apparently Brittany, with her ready smile and willingness for conversation, was often approached by guys in their hope of getting to know her. John T had been challenged and intrigued to understand Brittany better. In Britt's true style she'd often invite these guys for supper, to church and then perhaps even offer to share the work-benefits ski pass she had access to. One afternoon, Brittany had called home to ask me for the recipe for roasting a chicken that she wanted to serve in two hours to John and some other people. I explained to Britt about roasting the chicken for about two to three hours at 350, basting periodically, with an onion or apple inside the chicken for increased flavour or tenderness. "But Mom, how long if the chicken is still frozen?"

February 27, John had been with Britt's roommate at the Calgary airport waiting for our daughter to arrive on the flight she never made.

From my journal:

*** About 1 ½ wks ago John T from Australia phoned—he talked to Ralph. I could see Ralph tearing up as he talked. John chitchatted a bit and then wanted us to know about his sister Jan's dream. Jan had stayed with Brittany for a number of days when she came out to visit her brother John in Canmore. (Their grandmother had died about two years ago). So Jan had this dream ... Apparently she does not dream very often, however, this dream was so vivid she felt it was happening in real life. Apparently granny came to visit Jan. She explained in her rich Aussie accent that she just wanted to "pop by" and let Jan know that she (granny) had met "that Canadian girl from Canmore up here, her & I are becoming best of buddies." Just asked Ralph—this is what he recalls John as saying "I just popped by to let you know I've met a girl Brittany up here—she says she knows you & John. And we're just becoming the best of buddies." Then I heard Ralph saying all choked up, "Wow, I wish I could have a dream like that."

I wondered why John & Jan would get the dream and perhaps they needed it more than we did. And it was very neat to get this call from halfway around the world to let us know. Thank you Lord.

Speaking of dreams, about a week ago I dreamt I was pregnant with twins, a boy and a girl. I asked the Lord if He was joking. I realized He'd restored Job's family and fortune, but I am 50 yrs old—they'd be taking their drivers & I'd be 66, way too old for either Ralph or I to teach them. Asked God what kind of cruel joke that was. Thanks, but no thanks. Ralph & I kind of laughed about that one. ***

THIRD

We continued to wait for a sign or a dream, and one morning it had happened.

From my journal, dated May 6:

*** Had not mentioned Ralph's dream from last week Sat to Sun ....We were pretty tired going to bed. In the morning Ralph asked me, "Did you have a dream?" "No, did you?" "Yes!"

This is what his dream was: "All of a sudden Jordan was standing by my bed & talking to me, almost like he was trying to wake me up." Then he said, "Dad, look, Dad, Brittany's there, over there it's Brittany." So he looked and there was Britt sitting on our bed—kind of with her back to him, leaning over me, touching my leg saying (as if I had been very upset & I had been), "Hey Mom, it's ok, I'm fine, really I'm fine." Then Ralph realized—Hey that had been Jordan, so he looked back & he sees Jordan. Jordan gave him a huge smile & then kind of disappeared. He turned to see Britt and she kind of disappeared as well. Ralph noted she had her dreadlocks back and she was wearing a light blue hoody.

WOW! Thank you Lord. We'll hold on to that one. Ralph said this was about 4am. He wanted to wake me to see, but he couldn't move or speak. But in the morning I remembered waking up, hearing a noise and thinking something was happening in the room. It was as though I sensed a presence and it was the exact same time. I felt like I should look to the door to see something, but was unable to move. We told Curt & Deb the dream, they both had tears in their eyes. ***

FOURTH

People gave us books about those who'd had near death experiences, dreams, or visions. I started almost all the books given to me, but finished only the ones that were helpful. Another dream experience came from an aunt, and wonderful sister in the Lord. They had lost a son almost exactly two years before our accident.

From my journal:

*** *Ruth shared something that was obviously very hard for her. For the last year or so, she'd sometimes get an image of me standing over a coffin of a child. She was very upset over the image and begged God, "Please NO." She was so afraid we were going to lose Kristen. She had such great pain all over again, for us with this tragedy. I got goosebumps/shivers/tears when she told me this story. But somehow, it made events seem more planned and known, not just a freak accident. I'm not sure I can explain that. We had some good hugs and tears together.* ***

At the funeral, pastor Herb had challenged God with his own question, "Like what were you thinking, did you fall asleep at the wheel? ... Jordan and Brittany had so much life and love of God to share with the rest of the world, why, oh why God did you take them?"

For some reason, this concept of God having let someone else know that this tragedy was part of a bigger plan, even if we would never get to understand it ... brought an inexplicable comfort.

All the days ordained for me were written in your book before one of them came to be."

Ps 139:16 NIV

Who of you by worrying can add a single hour to his life?

Matt 6:27 NIV

FIFTH

I had been sick just prior to this dream and Ralph was in Winnipeg overnight. The dream was set in my childhood home, although I was an adult. In reality I had had a night sweat and looked at the clock at 5 am.

From my journal, Oct 1, 2005:

*** It's 6:15 am and I just had a dream and wanted it to be remembered. I was back in the house on 6th street south with Mom, in the second bedroom on the east side, long before the kitchen renovations. In my dream I was busy working on something & I heard a knock. Mom said she did the knock because she wanted me to know I had a visitor—it was also 5 am in my dream. So I went to the little bedroom and there is Jordan as a 9 or 10 year old boy. He's under the covers with his shy grin and a twinkle in his eye. I came to him and hugged him and then I was crying as I said,

"Oh Jordan something terrible has happened—someone has died but I don't know who it was—was it Grandma?"
No" I continued "it was Brittany," he just hugged me or let me still hold him.
"No, it was Brittany," I repeated ... slowly the realization came over me and I said
"And you Jordan—you died—why or how come you're here?"
He said something like, "I could come for a little while."
Then I started to ask him questions as if he was ten years old, "And how is it in heaven?" Initially he just said, "Yes, yes, yes, it is good."
Me—"Do you play sports up there?"

"Oh yeah, we have just amazing games to play." (He was dressed similarly to a picture I have of him, a big striped T-shirt, with a short hair cut, and his front hair was gelled up a bit—maybe he had a cap?)

All of a sudden I heard Rita (my sister) come, she wanted to add something to a poster we'd been working on, I was hoping she wouldn't come in the room, as if I knew he'd go then. And I wondered why she came at 5 in the morning? Mom told her Jordan was here and she shouldn't go in yet. I don't remember what else I asked Jordan. Rita popped her head in the door, "Just wanted to say hi"—he smiled at her and was gone. And then I really woke up at 5:50 am, holding on to a pillow that was wet with tear stains.

My mother heart just ached to hold my little boy again, but I told myself he wasn't a little boy anymore. Tears were still running down my cheeks and I felt such a loss, and then I thought—No God, I had wanted to have a dream and so I will try to take comfort in it. ***

The words underneath this story in my journal said,
    The Lord will give strength to his people
    the Lord will bless His people with peace.
and I had added beside that, *Please do, feel free to do that any time now.*

As I typed this almost five years later, even though I'd forgotten much of this incident, I felt the comfort I had with that "Hug from Heaven."

CHAPTER FIVE

GARDENING AND
THE FOUNTAIN

Following Mother's day, it became important for me to visit Kristen in Kenya. Both she and I were having difficulty coping. I wanted Ralph to come as well, but he felt he needed the routine of work to help him get through the days. There were times I felt incredibly sad for him; he looked so disheartened. We probably both did, and even if we thought we looked okay, there was a weariness that showed up in our eyes, that could not be easily disguised.

From my journal:

*** May 17. Yes I know I am not the only one suffering, but oh Lord, the pain and hurt is so unbelievable. It's been 11 wks now and everything seems more intensified than I could've thought possible. I feel like I don't know what to do with myself. Was speaking to the travel agent (re Kenya tickets) yesterday and she was going to call back to see if she could find flights, I said I'd be outside in the garden. When she called she said, "Oh, you're lucky." Funny that struck me, I've not been called lucky in the last 11 wks. I wanted to say — "Yes! Lucky I'm so dysfunctional I should be in the basket weaving program." Fortunately I didn't respond ... Have a wilting big cucumber plant in view.

Linda gave it to me for Mother's day. And now its either too windy or wet—it looks how I feel. Maybe I look like that too. I feel like I'm on the 'try to make it through 10 min at a time' program again. ***

From my journal, May 23, 2005:

*** May long weekend. Ralph & I joked "all our weekends are long." No, we weren't going away—hadn't usually in the past number of years and I liked to garden the May long. And this weekend was the same. Ralph had been to Decor Cabinets the day before to share his story and ask for support for the camp memorial project. Stan came by to say they'd had their meeting and all agreed to support it. They have a real neat way of doing business; they pray about it and then get together. Would be neat if Ralph & co-workers could do some praying together. ***

Often when we came home there were things left on the doorstep; people would bring jars of soup, a card, a note, fresh buns or home-made cookies. It was a sign of tremendous caring demonstrated in a very practical way and we appreciated the tangible evidence in those first months.

From my journal:

*** Fri when we got home Kris D had brought 2 rose bushes over & a very nice card saying, "What you probably don't need is another person to tell you to 'Hang in there.'" Inside— "so I'm just letting you know that I'm reminding God, to keep His hold on you" Very nice! ....Today I planted my rose garden. Britt had always thought we should turn the spot in front of the shed into a rose garden, now I did. It helps to have 6 rose bushes given to us in memory. People are still so nice—But everything still hurts way too much. Pain and missing of Jordan & Brittany is unbelievably great. Ralph & I are sitting out in the prayer corner, our roses are looking pretty nice.

Every day I still question and wonder did this really happen to us?? I can't imagine someone living through this—yesterday was 12 weeks since the accident and this Friday will be the 27—the 'official' 3 month mark'. (I'm going in to make some tea) ***

The intensity of everyday living, while wishing for something else, took a heavy toll on both of us. We needed life, breath and fresh air. I seemed to feel everything so metaphorically ... If the sun was shining, I felt God was trying to encourage me; when it was bleak, so was I. The grey days could happen easily, even when the sun was shining. There must have been hundreds of people praying for us. We would get random phone calls, sometimes from perfect strangers. Many of them had also lost a son or daughter; they felt a connection and a need to encourage us to keep on walking. The memorial project for the Winkler Bible Camp turned into a huge venture. Although it became more than we could handle at times, it gave Ralph and I a physical opportunity to work out some of our grief. I worried about him. As a few men shared with me, "Ralph is a fixer, like most men ... he wants to be able to fix this problem." There is nothing on earth that can *fix* the death of two children.

We were both trying to cope in any way that we could. Gardening was therapeutic for me. Some of my co-workers had given me a gift certificate from the local greenhouse where Brittany had worked for two summers. It delighted me that she had picked up on my love of gardening. I had this lovely memory of going to visit her in the greenhouse, where she was serving customers with a smile. A female shopper came to the counter with a six-pack of flowers, where one plant had wilted; without skipping a beat, Britt had offered a discount. She had a ready smile and willingness to impart gardening advice, even if she was unsure.

The second year she had done her gardening homework, and was able to advise with more authority. If asked if this should be planted in the sun or shade, she would give an answer. She fell in love with the plants and would bring home rejects to see if we could nurse them back to life. She would also read about a unique plant and want to purchase it for our garden. We tried various things, some worked and some did not. The nursery was such a great place for her to work. Both she and the garden were growing into something of great beauty. And now, long before she had fully blossomed, she was snuffed out.

The gardening became a mixed blessing, full of beauty along with painful reminders of our precious time together. Fortunately, only one person had expressed the thought, "I guess God needed another gardener in Heaven." I think I was ready to hit anyone if they said that to me. God did *not* need any gardener. He planted the Garden of Eden all on His own—but me, I *needed* my gardener. I felt a connection to her while working with the plants. As we'd been given this gift certificate, I wanted to choose something more permanent for my garden from the greenhouse. We decided upon a fountain, which we had seen in a few places, but wanted to buy from the greenhouse that had employed her.

From my journal:

*** *Right now I'm sitting in the back yard—sound of running water, it could all be so peaceful and wonderful, IF ONLY ... Therein lies the trouble IF ONLY ... Those struggles have barely left for more than 30 minutes at any given time. Thankfully there are moments of sleep.*

Friday marked the official 3 month date. We decided on the fountain to commemorate Britt & Jordan; I told Ralph it didn't matter that it was $60 more at Foothills, I said that is where we needed to buy it. I went to pay and arrange for delivery. While paying, Sherri asks Holly was it $399 or $349? (Previously quoted $399) She looks at her papers and said $349. That was a bonus for doing the right thing. But then Sherri tells me, that for the last two years Brittany had set up this fountain and that it had been her favourite one. I could've cried. That was such a nice addition. One more bittersweet event. The fountain is also called The Ruin, more symbolism. Anyway, they delivered it Sat morning and Ralph had to take off, but all the pieces were in the right corner of the back yard. Ralph left & said he'd help me when he got back from work about 4:30. Well it was only 10:20 — what would make anyone think I would wait that long?? So I levelled the dirt, dug out the area, put the cement sidewalk tile down & proceeded to put it together. Took some maneuvering as it was way too heavy for me, but it all worked, (good body mechanics and some rolling of heavy pieces into place). Finally about noon, I'd filled it up, just plugged it in and up rides (my sister) Rita on her bike. Thank you for that added blessing of perfect timing. I mixed us a drink in wine glasses and we toasted, prayed over and dedicated the water fountain. It is beautiful in the wild flower garden. The top pillar has 4 spouts, different symbolisms — one each for Britt, Jord & Jamie and the fourth one for the rest of us left behind. Also father, son, Holy Ghost, and then us humans. Rita's timing was divinely appointed.

This past week I can see the strain on Ralph, it's like he's stressed about work, camp project and life. (Well that should be no surprise) He just doesn't voice it like me. He made a comment about everybody needing him at work also, I was thinking I should try not to rely on him. And I do try not to, I do have a good network of support with females. But the week before he had dreamed that he's gone far away all by himself

47

to start a new life—he said he felt like that sometimes. But so do I. ***

From my journal:

*** Since our whole episode, someone has confided in Ralph a lot ... all of a sudden I worried a bit ... Unfortunately too many stories of loss where the supporter and supported get into unhealthy unplanned attractions ... OK, I'm even kind of silly to write this down in my journal. But be on guard-because the adversary, the devil seeks only to destroy us. And what a good way—by seeking to destroy our marriage. Oh Lord, I love Ralph so much & have been so thankful for him. ***

Little bits of worries started to creep in ... the statistics for a marriage surviving the loss of children were not good. Surely this was not to be our case. Not us Lord.

From my journal:

*** Life seems so unreal now. I feel like my life is composed of a thousand clichés, only now they are true and I'm living it. Not actually living it—I'm in a movie scene—watching it and then I find out I'm one of the main characters.

Lord I just don't see how we can make it. Last night—we felt we might make it. The book says this is normal. Yeah it's one thing to make it through the grieving process; but when I think of the future, that is not going to be. What do we do with that Lord??

Somehow Lord you will need to rescue us and give us hope. ***

CHAPTER SIX

LESSONS FROM AFRICA— SHARING IN THE WORLDWIDE EXPERIENCE OF SUFFERING.

How can one know that a daughter will be taken away so suddenly and without warning? What would we do differently if we had known? I would have taken Brittany to Africa with us in 2004, had we known. She wanted to visit her sister in Kenya, but at the time we went, it was not feasible. Now I was going to Kenya for the second time and I felt guilty, guilty that I hadn't taken Britt there.

From my journal, June 1, 2005:

*** *So here we are, well actually here I am—in an airplane en route to London – Nairobi – Mombasa. I'm sipping a glass of white wine, starting a movie, National Treasure and I think some food will be served soon. Seems as though life should be good—if only—if only, THAT IS THE BIG ONE. This morning as I was trying to finalize stuff, I wanted to take something of Britt's to Africa, as if it would symbolically make up for her not getting to come, it's all so unreal that she is gone and Jordan, too—man ... anyway ... This is life now. I was going to wear a sweater of hers, but it felt too small. I realized she probably* *wouldn't know or care, but as I sat in the car I began to cry. I wanted to take something of hers, and then my hand went to the New Testament of hers I'd picked up to read en route. I just said, Thank you Lord, how much better to take the Word than a stuffed toy or a sweater. (I had almost made Ralph go home to pick up a stuffed toy to bring to Africa.)* ***

Britt had loved stuffed animals and had collected quite a few over the years. They were arranged somewhat lovingly or haphazardly depending on the amount of time she had. I was reminded again of my brother-in-law's wise words: that we had to live *our* lives, we could not and should not try to live our kids' dreams for them. They were already in a far better place.

An African church service

From my journal:

*** *Sunday June 4, 2005. Well Britt, your New Testament and small travel bag made it to Kenya; both are here in K&K's church this morning. We've just had some singing, prayer request time and testimony. Kristen encouraged me to get up and say something. So I did a greeting and said the Lord has walked with us, the last time we came was more joyful. Mayo Naomi had an African blessing for me—she is a wonderful lady. A big warm smile and we can see the love of Jesus in her. Kristen told me much of her story; the lady has suffered a lot and it certainly is the joy of the Lord in her. We've been in church an hour and a half. And I'm feeling pretty tired right now, jet lag and exhaustion probably. Kristen pointed out a girl who is 2 ½ yrs old and just learned to walk. She had cerebral malaria about age one and still does not talk. Thank you Lord for the breeze blowing through right now, and this is winter.*

Just went out of church for a breath of fresh air. The pastor Dette, is giving some very animated stories of faith. Very *expressive. I can just imagine Jordan & Britt laughing together with us (us not understanding—but the pastor's going on & on in Chiduruma language about—"a shittein-alleluia").* ***

The singing in this African church was like no other I'd ever heard. When Ralph and I were here the previous fall, we had been fascinated by the high-pitched ululating sounds that some of the ladies made as they sang, as seen in African movies. This day the enthusiasm was evidenced by clapping, swaying, and smiling faces. The drum had been replaced, as a hungry dog had eaten the leather skin that had been pulled tight to make a drum. This drummer did a great job beating out a fast and steady rhythm on the plastic pail that served as the replacement. They were just announcing an official 'sorry time/firaja' at Nadzuwa's (Kristen's African name) house this Wednesday. I wondered what would happen then? The sorry time was announced in honour of my being there, a way to acknowledge the sorrow Kristen and I had experienced. Somehow, a fifty-year-old (white) woman was raised to celebrity status; they actually honoured older people here. Kristen and Kevin, along with their team members, were also granted celebrity status, because they have journeyed farther than Nairobi and traveled by plane. Most of these people have not moved beyond the borders of their village or district area. Few people owned a vehicle and public transport was used only when absolutely necessary.

Interesting that neither wealth nor poverty offered exemptions, when it came to sorrow and suffering. These people understood the concept of sharing the sorrow, and for that reason they planned this 'sorry' event for me/us.

Note of explanation: Kristen was given the name Nadzuwa in Swahili, and Kevin was given the name Mlalla. Both were common names; Nadzuwa meant "with sun" and Mlalla referred to a strong reed that was used in the weaving of mats. The lady who did laundry for them, was also named Nadzuwa.

Next journal entry:

*** *Today is Monday June 5/05—in Kenya. This is the right place to be. Talked to Ralph on the phone last night – Good to hear him. He still feels so overwhelmed with everything. Like, how is it that my Jord & Britt are gone? And yet here most parents have lost a child it seems. (But not two out of three.)* ***

From my journal:

*** *The Lord will fulfill his purpose for me; Your Love, O Lord, endures forever—do not abandon the work of your hands. Ps 138:8 NIV God stay with us.*

Noonish—we've had a good/full morning. K & I went for a good long walk, met various people along the way, picked up 2 rocks to take back with me, came back to have Chai tea with Nadzuwa, the wash lady. Kevin shared the kid's story of the 5 loaves and 2 fishes with her, as she was checking out the crafts on the wall. It has been so good to be a part of seeing their everyday life. Received a few "sorry, sorry" and "make sure your mother is eating" comments to Kristen. Such a mixture of emotions. A bit of joy, but then quickly questioning as to, should I even be allowed to feel joy.

I see Jord, Britt & Jamie's pictures here in K&K's home and it feels so overwhelming—but K& I decided on our walk today that, the intensity has lessened, but the pain is still huge. Nadzuwa, the lady who does wash for Kristen, had some neat insights for the old Mayo neighbour. The old Mayo, Mayo refers to 'mother', in this case the old Mayo is the first of seven wives of Baba Nyenge's family. In this little family structure unit, she is the most respected and the eldest of the wives, (the youngest is 27 and has a two year old baby). Mayo says to Kristen "Tell your mother she should be eating."

Nadzuwa replies, "her spirit is still so sad she cannot eat." These people do know about death and suffering, they usually expect that white people do not. For them part of it is that children are valued, not so much as individuals, but as a source of support in your old age. (There are not too many senior or retirement care homes here.) ....

(later same day) Wow, what an amazing day, this afternoon was a real blessing. We went to visit a lady who gave birth 2 days ago. It was a sister-in-law to the wash lady Nadzuwa. (We walked along red dusty trails through the scrub brush land, passing the odd small group of people out in the fields or kids playing soccer, with a ball made of plastic strips wound together.) Kristen loaded 2 baskets full of gifts to bless the new mom with: flour, sugar, oil, some seeds to plant, crackers, 2 bars of soap, a kid sized T-shirt, & the dress that a co-worker had sent along. But wow — we went to her 2-room hut, there were two beds in the one room and one bed in the other. By bed, I mean a handmade wood frame with ropes across to hold the grass reed mat in place. She shared the bed with her newborn and 1½ yr old. Her older 2 children slept in the other bed. She let me hold her baby girl, a beautiful little one, prob 6 ½ lbs. Kristen translated as I asked questions.

There is something powerful and connecting about the universal nature of giving birth. She said she'd had no problems, she gave birth in the evening — no exact time — I wonder if they even know what date it is. As she experienced her pains, she had been walking back and forth outside her hut and gave birth outside as well. She stated she did it by herself — Kristen says that is usually the way it is, unless there are problems. Her mother-in-law had come to cut the cord with a brand new knife. I looked and saw there was some kind of rope for tying. How neat to share her story. Kristen told me I had asked great questions. I also told the lady a number of times, "what a beautiful baby." The baby was quite dark — DUH!! — but Kristen said newborns are often fairly light, and will darken within a week. The ladies desire the more pale kids, for some reason. The hair was also soft and straight which will probably change after a month or so, when they razor off the baby hair.

Within 5 min of us being there, all the neighbor kids crowded into the little room, at least 11 of them and a few other women came as well. It was really quite the experience. (Amazing to me how some of the ladies made almost rude comments re the baby being dark — not desired, and that seemed weird to me. That is why I wanted to impart to this lady, a sense of the beautiful treasure she had, in this brand new baby. I felt saddened for the future difficult life this child would probably grow into, and yet, the power of holding a newborn baby in my arms was a gift.) Again this morning, as we saw the baby goats being separated from their mamas for the day, while they went off to pasture. We saw them being reunited after the day, it made me feel so sad. I was a momma goat, whose babies didn't come back.

Oh Lord, I will never get to share birthing stories with Brittany or Jamie.

Later in the afternoon, we stopped at Gwede's and Keenyavo's (other neighbours). We were just doing some idle chitchat, and then they made a comment that triggered something. (Kristen had to interpret.) I told the wife, if it had not been for our tragedy, I probably would not be here again. So then we got talking about tragedy & I asked if they'd suffered the loss of a *child. (It seems many have.) Yes they had. Their daughter was 18, at secondary boarding school not very far away. She got sick there and died, and the way Keenyavo was informed was when they brought her daughter's body to her house. Oh that must've been hard!! We shared in the "fellowship of suffering." I told her through Kristen, if it hadn't been for the Lord's help I would never make it. Keenyavo told me she never left her housing complex for 2 years, not even to go to the store. Wow, that also was quite a powerful time. There are many people who have lost a child, a sibling or both, but I do not know if they have the hope of seeing them in the next life. Our hope of eternity really, really is a comfort. It does not make the pain go away, but I am so thankful for the hope of reunion.*

(Kristen met regularly with 3 ladies for a mini teaching session and had asked if I would share something.) I shared verses from the funeral. From Lamentations 2:19. Arise cry out in the night ... Pour out your heart like water ... for the lives of your children. We poured out some water from our 'tupa' (jug), then read the verses about God's faithfulness, His hope and His mercy. We shared the concept of a mother's heart— whether we are black, or white—our desires for our children are similar. We prayed together and the most touching comments were that, if they had been able to they would've come to Canada to say sorry. ***

I received many greetings of sorry sorry; in their language the words were: *pore, pore.* The church and community had the official *firaja* visit midweek for Kristen and me, even though some politics got involved in the decision to do this. For instance, the church was just starting to do official bereavement visits and this was the first one; the question came up whether to serve food or not? We would have gladly served, but then they felt it set a standard too high that might be hard for others to follow. I didn't care much one way or the other. It seemed interesting to realize that the devil was in the details out here as well. Overall, it was a very moving experience and I think the decision to not serve food was the right one. It would've placed too much focus on the wrong thing.

There was some singing, scripture and then people were allowed to share words of encouragement for us. Kristen had told me to be prepared to receive gifts of money, as that is their way of expressing condolences. I guess not unlike 'the damn flowers.' For this culture money is most practical and acceptable. I experienced a genuine connection, on a deep level with these people, in their land, with their strange language. Together we identified in the universality of suffering.

> The APOLOGY
> Pore Pore
> (Sorry sorry)
> So sorry for your loss.
> Mom, they will try to give you money.
> This is their way of showing sympathy.
> Be gracious and take it. So I did.
> She stands apart.
> Mouths are moving
> Voices are heard and not heard,
> A prayer is spoken in Swahili
> And the Voice of God seems
> the only Silent One.
> And perhaps He is.
> She wonders does God ever say Sorry?
> (Or does He just understand, and wish things
> weren't so?)

From my journal:

*** *June 8, 2005 Looking at the pictures on the wall of the smiling faces of Jordan, Jamie & Britt. It still is an everyday question—Did this really happen? Kristen shared with me that she feels like she doesn't want to come back to Canada—but I told her she has no idea how much dad is looking forward to that. That is a real encouragement for her. But I can see the beauty of being here—the world is so different, you do get to live a different life, just like Ralph & I want to. And for me it will be the going home that is difficult. I got tears and felt like weeping when I saw the calendar Brittany & I sent Kristen for Christmas. To see all the personal notes we'd included, especially the mark for October 2005, with a BIG FEHR FAMILY REUNION!! marked in bold. A mocking reminder of what is not ever going to be again.* ***

As much as there had been sorrow mixed with joy in Kenya, I had ambivalent emotions for the return home. Here in Africa circumstances were so different, and it was an opportunity to avoid the pain for a while. I dreaded the return to the bleakness of the reminders of my *new life*.

FATHER'S DAY

It seemed as though Ralph had sunk even lower while I was in Kenya. It made me feel guilty for having gone, and yet I knew I needed to do it for myself and for Kristen.

Grief is a very dark and lonely pathway.

From my journal:

*** *I've never seen Ralph like this. He has such a look of sadness, I said to someone—Always in Ralph's life, he could resolve almost anything, by a greater effort, working harder, he has always been self-reliant. Lord you have broken him, please help build him up again ... Thank you for people who still* *encourage us. Lianne sent us a nice card for Father's Day. Carol and Holly came by on the Sat before Father's day and gave Ralph a nice card. "Missing you on Father's Day" it said. Holly wrote on the inside, "I don't have a dad to wish Happy Father's Day to—so I'm wishing you one—you're an awesome father!" Oh Holly that was so meaningful. She reminds me of Britt in many ways ... Lord love that girl & be a father to her, and keep Carol in your care as well. ****

Further pain came for Ralph on Father's Day. Somehow we felt we should and could bravely host his family for a Father's Day BBQ. By the end of the evening I was so disappointed ... not one person said anything to Ralph about this being a difficult day for him, the first Father's Day, and the loss so fresh, not one. The few times he or I mentioned Jordan or Brittany, there was no follow up from anyone else. It felt as though they just did not know how to empathize this day.

As the evening progressed, we continued to talk about the family farm, the possibility that the new owners wanted to turn it into an auto wrecking place, and how disgusting that would be ... someone else discussed the possibility for their care group doing dance lessons.

Perhaps we had set ourselves up for failure. The evening was a disappointment for us; we were both waiting for our guests to leave. That day it would have been better to be with strangers who did not know our situation, than to be with people who knew, and did not know how to acknowledge the pain. The difficult challenge for those around people experiencing grief is for them to be willing to discuss, to be willing to listen, rarely to offer advice, and to discern what is needed for the moment.

Sometimes the elephant in the room is so big that it consumes all the oxygen and there is no hope of the disabled ones to catch a breath.

From my journal:

*** *They either had no idea how much pain we were in — or they just don't know how to communicate or express concern. I think I received more empathy from the neighbour's cat.* ***

Before I had gone to Africa, I sensed that Ralph was going down into a pit. I spoke to our pastor and asked if he could come alongside Ralph, or have some men come to support him. I felt he needed godly men, some men to help him bear the load, guys with whom to do stuff: golf, talk, go for coffee. When I returned it was mid-June, churches slow down and almost come to a standstill for the summer. It seemed to me that Ralph was put on the shelf, perhaps until the fall. There's an Eric Clapton song that has a line: "*Nobody knows you when you're down and out, everyone wants to be your long lost friend when things are fine, but nobody knows you when you're down and out.*"

In many ways, women have an easier time expressing emotions. We can allow our emotions to be visible. We are expected to be emotional. I was disappointed with God and man for not being there for my husband. Some needs I could not help him with.

"*Sudden and tragic loss leads to terrible darkness. It is as inescapable as nightmares during a high fever. The darkness comes, no matter how hard we try to hold it off. However threatening, we must face it, and we must face it alone.*"

Gerry Sittser in *Grace Disguised*

CHAPTER SEVEN

REFLECTIONS FROM THE STATE OF GRIEF:

Could I change my address?

I would like to live in a different state.

They say that the first year of grief is the hardest, to navigate all the special events and holidays without your loved one. Time had so little meaning. Things seemed to happen too quickly and still in slow motion. Little events came up that totally blindsided me and emotionally took me down for a while. I learned to live in a mode of self-protection, avoided conversations and events I thought could be painful. But, at this early stage of grief, all of life was difficult. There were many days where just breathing was a major accomplishment.

People would ask, "So... how are you doing?" My cerebral response: "Do you really want to know?" This query became very difficult for me. I had long hated that question, and I knew it should only be regarded as a politeness. None the less, it had always seemed rude to me if people asked the "How are you?" without waiting for an answer. All they wanted was to hear "Good." But that was an outrageous lie. Did they really want to know? We came to realize that people wanted us to be good for their sakes, as much as for ours.

They wanted the answer *good*, so that they could stop feeling badly for us. "As well as can be expected," became the standard answer. And not surprisingly most people did not pursue it. At one point it became a little black-humoured challenge for me to come up with answers to shock people, who unwittingly asked the question. In that mind-frame, my response varied from: "Like have you got an hour?" Or, "I'm trying to join Jordan and Brittany." Or Do you really want to know?" Or, "Feels like shit, do you want to know more?" The one that confirmed lack of sincerity, came when a coworker asked me the "So, how are you doing?" with heavy emphasis on *so*. I said "*Nasoha*," an African term I had picked up in Kenya that meant: I am barely breathing. To which she efficiently replied, "Oh, that's good."

What I really wanted to shout at them was, "How do you think I am doing? I've lost two kids and my life is not going well! I'm struggling to make it through the day,"... but I didn't answer that because it would cause me more pain than I could handle. Even some of the people closest to me had difficulty understanding my reluctance to being out in public, until a sister was in the store and she was mistaken for me. Between being asked in a pained way, "Are you Jocelyn?" to having *that look*, she told me, she could now understand. I detested the pitying looks. It was not empathy, it was pity reflected in their eyes, and a sense of the 'I need to pray for that woman,' or 'Oh my goodness, I'm so thankful it is not me.' I hated being the person who no one wanted to be.

I did not want to be me.

The working out of my faith

There is an underlying belief among many Christians, whether stated or not, that though difficulties may come to your life—after all, the rain falls on the just and the unjust—the people of faith should get over it more quickly. Even more damaging is the prosperity gospel and its offshoot beliefs in which the tenet of faith is that because one is a believer, God wants to bless you and give you health and happiness. As other Christians pray, thanking God for His blessings of His presence, His mercy, good health, stable marriages, smiling children; those who are struggling in any of these areas, can come to the ill-founded conclusion, that God is not involved in their lives and has removed His blessing from them. The following assumption is that either you do not have enough faith, or your circumstances are a punishment or trial from God. Therefore, you should examine your life, confess your sin or pray for increased faith; and you will be brought to health and well-being again. The belief is that because we have the *power* of God in us and at our disposal, we should be stronger than mere mortal human beings. My life felt like a constant battleground for the struggle between humanity and divinity.

One difficult question I faced was, *How much control did I have?* Was there really anything I could do that would make any difference?

Never in all my life had I grasped the burden of what the proverbial fall from grace had done to humanity and the reality of the pain of brokenness.

And never before had the strength and beauty of the Lord become so evident in my life.

Unless the Lord had given me help, I would soon have dwelt in the silence of death.

When I said, "My foot is slipping," your love, O Lord, supported me.

When anxiety was great within me, your consolation brought joy to my soul. Psalm 94:17-19 NIV

(In the margins of my Bible I had written—I'm not just slipping Lord, I'm falling.)

All the clichés, beautiful promises and challenges to rise up, everything fell so flat. I struggled under the weight of it all. Ralph and I felt that the eyes of the community were upon us. Unfortunately, in many ways the church is less supportive of people struggling—although we easily rejoice with those who have overcome. As a church we flounder to support the people long term, who have been given a load that is too heavy to bear.

At times people wanted to offer encouragement or blessing through various Scripture verses, but sometimes those verses, either misquoted or misunderstood, added further confusion or heartache. From Paul's words in 1 Corinthians the concept arises that "God only gives as much as we are able to handle."

No temptation has seized you except what is common to man. And God is faithful; he will not let you be tempted beyond what you can bear. But when you are tempted He will also provide a way out so that you can stand up under it. 1 Corinthians 10:13 NIV

No test or temptation that comes your way is beyond the course of what others have had to face. All you need to remember is that God will never let you down; he'll never let you be pushed past your limit; he'll always be there to help you come through it." 1 Corinthians 10:13 The Message

From my journal:

*** *OK, Rita (sister) was telling me something I disagree on. She and her daughter were talking. Rita told her, "God gives these hard things to people with lots of faith." Well I disagree! In some ways things are random, and yet not—but non-Christians have difficulties and so do the Christians—both the weak and the strong ones. God wants to provide support as* *we walk the road, but I don't think it's Biblical to say stronger Christians get the tough times. (That could be a great argument for remaining weak in faith?) Tough times do make stronger believers—but also can make or break anyone. ****

When someone told me that we "are not given more than we can handle," my mind wanted to *scream* at anyone who thought I could handle what I had been dealt!! I did respond adamantly though that this was *way* more than I could handle. I also thought those scriptures were often misquoted. In the Banff Park Church, we had heard a message that helped clarify this for me.

From my journal:

*** The pastor said, "God is our comfort, He is all we need. Some of our suffering is given so we do not rely on ourselves but on God." He also talked about the oft misquoted verse, 1 Cor 10:13 where it says, "we will not receive more temptation than we can bear." That refers to temptation, not suffering. Yes we do receive suffering more than we can bear—that is to allow the comfort of God to come and heal us. (from pastor Norm's message)

LORD WE ARE GOING TO HOLD YOU TO YOUR WORD. ***

When Paul experienced great difficulty, he confessed to being "under great pressure, far beyond our ability to endure, so that we were despaired even of life." (New International Version 2 Cor 1:8.)

Well, I could identify with that, including being despaired even of life.

I hunted for scripture to assure me, strengthen me and just hold me ... and in it all, I experienced a more personal and powerful God, who loved me. The God who entered humanity, because He could see it was too messed up. He came to be among us, as one of us.

The most comforting people in my journey were not the ones who tried to provide answers, but those who recognized that some things have no answer. Genuine support came from those who spent time with me, those who were willing to let me voice my questions and my struggles. It is not the answers given that are important in this process; it is being willing to *explore and validate the journey of the question.* In the face of immense tragedy, band-aid scripture is not meant to be liberally applied.

When I was quoted verses about God, my loving Father, I wanted to say as an imperfect parent, I would not do this to my child. Where is the love in all of this? Academically, I was aware that we are His and we cannot understand, and that death is a result of living in a fallen world, but most often my truest response was, "I believe, help me in my unbelief."

That first summer we saw a counsellor for one visit. He listened with some empathy, but told us, "Don't grieve too long. Get out and do something good for someone else. If you get involved with other people and their difficulties, it will help you in your situation. Get beyond yourself." It sounded good, in theory. The only positive from this visit was the poster he had in his room: a picture of an ocean storm, in dark shades of blue, with huge waves crashing. You could sense the power of the storm. The words printed above were:

Don't tell God how big your storm is ...

Tell the storm how big Your God is.

We went away feeling somewhat flat. Over the summer, I could feel Ralph pull away from me, and sink deeper into a hole, trying to use work as his coping mechanism. It seemed as though that talk legitimized Ralph to get involved in the helping out situation of a female who struggled with significant difficulties in her own life. Whatever satisfaction he received from helping her, became difficult for me, especially as I felt I needed his support. Emotionally he withdrew, choosing to utilize his energies in an area where he felt he could actually do something about the problem.

I spoke to a friend who had also lost a child, about the distancing between Ralph and myself. She told me that she and her husband had hardly been able to make it with the loss of one child. "Joc, I don't see how you can make it losing two children." That was not encouraging. Another friend said, "Oh Joc and Ralph have a good marriage and a strong faith; they'll be ok."

How could anyone even say that when they had no possible clue of our struggles? I was feeling the strain on our relationship. It was like watching a child drowning and being helpless to do anything.

I could not fathom that this pain of marital distancing would be added to the rest of the heap; this was more than I could bear. I needed my husband more than ever and the pressure mounted for both of us. Not only had I lost my two children, it felt as if I was losing my husband.

Ralph seemed to understand my struggle, but I felt he did not choose to do the things that would have been beneficial for our relationship. He became defensive about his actions, and I remained mostly silent wanting to believe him, praying all the harder for us. I was like the pit bull, fighting tenaciously for my marriage, hanging on with the desperation the dog has when he grabs hold of an object, thrashing it about in an effort to hold on. We each had our own journey. The song *Lonesome Valley* reminded me that nobody could walk it for me or for Ralph ... we had to walk it for ourselves.

The pain and pressure of grief wore us down, until it seemed we were only reminders of our sorrows when we were together. That summer was excruciating in many ways ... but we looked forward to Kristen and Kev's return from Africa. Ralph increasingly spoke of either going away or moving out of the house. He assured me that if we did separate, I should always know it had nothing to do with me. That did not bring me any comfort.

I read a saying somewhere—among the abundance of sayings and quotes I read—that claimed, "What you find will usually be what you are looking for," or "What you find, depends on what you are looking for." It was apparent that Ralph and I were looking at our lives through different lenses. Bizarre and unusual incidents came to both of us in our journey. It seemed that people who had gone through tragedy with subsequent marriage breakups all came to talk to him that summer; from a customer two provinces away, to a lady who sent him an article on how to get through a breakup. Probably the story that Ralph connected with most was the one he heard on the radio. A man had been involved in an accident that left him a paraplegic. This man decided that the only way for him to move on and overcome this great loss was to commit emotional suicide. He needed to envision his death, and then a rebirth, leaving all the old behind.

It was an intense summer. In some ways, the pain of marital distance became greater for me than the pain of the loss of our children. It was not a choice our children had made for themselves and I felt my husband could choose. In actuality, the cumulative effect of all the sorrow and loss became too much, depleting both of us physically and emotionally. My heart ached for him and longed for him. It was a very, very dark place to be.

RALPH'S SECOND DREAM

Ralph had a second dream. The scenario was at a mealtime, likely at Christmas. My recollection of his telling of the dream is that both he and I sat at the festive table with different partners. Kristen and Kevin were also present. Jordan and Brittany arrived late and Jordan might have been the only one to speak. Apparently, no one seemed to think it odd that Ralph or I had different partners. Because of that, I *hated* this dream and felt that it could not have had any authenticity. I remembered two things about Ralph's sharing of the dream. Jordan made a comment about us "getting things all wrong, ... you have no idea who's all up here." He also spoke some words to his dad, something like, "Mom really needs you now (?for a while)." In the daytime, I challenged him with that one, especially Jordan's words to Ralph about me needing him. But I also wanted to apply legalistic and theological arguments to his dream.

What I disliked about this dream, were the feelings it invoked within me and my unwillingness to accept what Ralph felt was the intended message. I realized he interpreted it differently than I did. It was probably more a relief for him, in that his sense was that our marriage was fatally wounded and his only hope was to move on, possibly with another partner.

And how can you argue with someone else's dream??

On October 3, 2005, Ralph told me that he needed to leave the house and me for a few days stating his "head was just too messed up." He needed space to breathe. He termed this temporary. This was six days before Kristen and Kevin were due to arrive back from Kenya.

From my journal:

*** Well, well It's Wed Oct 5th 8am and it is snowing outside.
I see all my garden plants—I didn't prepare for this and just
hope the fountain won't freeze or the fish in the pond. But in
the grand scheme of things, who cares? All the leaves are still on
our backyard trees. I don't think I'm ready for an early winter,
feels like it could be the winter of my soul. Just heard a song
on a CD from Debbie, Be Thou my Vision. I've always liked that
song and ask now Lord that you could be our vision, that you
give us a vision of how to keep on going, of being renewed—
For without a vision the people perish. Jordan would have been
so excited to see the snow, he always liked winter. And Britt—
she and her friends would've started hauling snow to Morden
to make some jumps for snow-boarding. I'm sipping a frothy
cup of mocha chocolate—nope actually French Vanilla. Glad
I can stay at home today.

I had a strange dream of sorts, can't quite remember it. It
was windy & sounding stormy and I woke from the sound,
I thought someone was in the room. I looked up and thought
Ralph is that you?—then I tried to speak those words aloud.
And then a 6 to 8 yr old Brittany came in the room because she
was afraid of the storm. She wanted to climb into bed with
me as she asked, "Where's dad?" I said, "He's still at work," to
which she said "he should be here." And that seemed to end
it. You're right Britt, he should be here. Just read a quote from
Max Lucado:

"If God has been with you this far, He's not going to leave you
when you're in troubled times. If your faith has brought you
this far, don't throw it out when the going gets tough."

Ps 42:11 Why are you downcast Oh my soul, put your hope in
God for I will yet praise Him.

Cleaned up Jordan's broken guitar from downstairs. It was in the car at the accident and is irreparable. We've just left so much for so long—cuz I don't know what to do with it—keep it or throw it away? ***

The guitar symbolized so much, like our marriage, it had been something which had produced beautiful music. Jordan had been composing his own song and I had been the only one privileged to hear it, his own composition. I could picture him playing it ... his strong kind hands moving the strings to create such beautiful music ... and now the guitar, like my life and marriage, had been *smashed to bits*. There were too many pieces; it would not be salvageable.

Oh Lord, put a song in my heart.

CHAPTER EIGHT

IF YOU DON'T LAUGH, YOU WILL CRY

I chose to look at the bright side whenever I could.
God still maintained some sense of humour in horrible times.

PERCEPTION
She needs new glasses.
I look at my life through anorexic eyes
the pain and the loss give the wrong size.
Inside of me, a peaceful soul is waiting to
leap out
Needing to be cajoled
Give me laughter
Happy ever after.
Others see me as gaunt and thin
Anxiety ridden, struggling to win
Help me see through your eyes
the richness of Life
My perception is hard to shake
Enough *is enough, Let's do a retake.*
Open the eyes of my heart, Lord

I want to see you
And know you in all this pain.

What to do with belongings was a dilemma. If we were just going through the ordinary kids leave home phase it, would not have been such a big deal. Yes, you can get sentimental over all the baby things, but we suddenly felt as if we needed to hold on to everything, because it was all we had. Not only that, it was just too painful to spend any amount of time sorting through stuff, to figure out what to keep and what to discard. There were sporadic efforts to clean up their rooms. One day, after I had done some organizing and sorting, Ralph and I lit a bonfire in the back yard, and put many of their personal items in the flames, in some sort of symbolic closure. We knew we could not keep coming across certain bits and pieces, as it was too painful.

GIRL YOU GOTTA PROTECT YOURSELF

Life became an obstacle course. An enormous amount of energy was expended trying to protect myself, to keep myself from potentially hazardous situations and that included almost everything. I was looking at life through a totally different set of glasses. I was extremely sensitive to words that put a knife in my heart. The ads on TV, "Buy one, get one free" or the "two for one deal" caused my heart to recoil. My head was home to an ongoing dialogue/argument in response to my surroundings.

I tried to avoid the public or went to places where I was not known, even for grocery shopping; especially for grocery shopping, because everyone I knew also frequented either of the town's two stores. Now that Ralph had left temporarily, and who knew how long temporary was, I saw couples in the supermarket together and I longed for Ralph to come shopping with me. Hello girl, I said to myself, we rarely shopped together. Okay, maybe occasionally, but not usually. Normally, I did the main shopping and he'd just pick up a few needed things on the way home. Now, I saw overweight, unattractive women and their husbands pushing overloaded grocery carts and I envied them. Now the carts reminded me that I had no children to expect home for meals, and no husband to shop with.

Then I experienced this one event that really set me back. I had finally worked up the courage to get my own groceries, at the local Superstore. My shopping cart had a few items and I was just coming back for something near the entrance, when I heard a large booming voice coming from an equally large booming man, who looked vaguely familiar.

"Jocelyn, Jocelyn Fehr," he called out loudly enough to cause a few other people to look in our direction ... "Oh no ... just run away ... this is not sounding good," I thought. As he closed in on me, he used my maiden name "Jocelyn, Jocelyn Krahn, you're the one; you're the one who just lost her kids in the accident." He announced it with such vocal enthusiasm; you would think I had won the six million dollar lottery. "Yeah, I had to look it up in my high school yearbook when I heard about your accident. I was in the grade ahead of you. I checked it out. I'm so and so, we're just in town visiting my brothers. Just want you to know we're praying for you." I muttered something in reply, walked out of the store leaving my purchases behind, went to my vehicle and sat behind the steering wheel. It took five minutes to let the tears subside before I could drive home. There is a time and place for everything. That was not the time, place, or way for anyone to comfort those in need.

Consequently, I started doing regular shopping trips to Winnipeg, a city about 100 kilometres away.

Anonymity provided some relief.

RETAIL THERAPY and TRAVELLING ROUTES

I knew in my head it would not work for the long term, but I could not think long term.

I just needed to do something, *anything* to help me deal with short intervals. I would often go into Winnipeg, do some shopping, visit the park, and spend the day. It wasn't the worst coping mechanism I could've used—better than drugs I thought. Three main routes lead to Winnipeg. The first one was the road our children traveled that fateful day; the second most common was the route Ralph and I had taken that evening, as we rushed in to the hospital. That left me with the least used path and a bit of a roundabout way to get to Winnipeg. One day travelling with my mother, as we got to the intersection between the most used and the least used road, she asked "Aren't you going to turn here?"

"No."

"Don't you think you will ever drive there again?"

"Mom, my kids were killed on that road. I don't know *if* and *when* I will go there. This road only takes five minutes longer and this is the road we are driving on."

Some things we can choose; some things we cannot. It felt there was so little I could control, so I chose to take the least painful route in to Winnipeg. Who among us should try to tell a griever which road they should take, or when they are ready for it?

During my shopping excursions, I sometimes bought clothing that I would later question—why had I purchased that? I'm sure all of my sisters received at least one piece of new clothing bought in a moment of retail therapy.

CHAPTER NINE

FALL(ING)

When you can't trace his hand, you can trust His heart.
Charles H. Spurgeon

Mid-October 2005. Kristen and Kevin had only been back from Africa about five days. My greatest fear was that I did not want Kristen to find out that her dad was not living with me, but it became increasingly difficult, as she dropped by at odd hours to see *us*. I felt I was living a lie, and was ashamed that our marriage was coming apart and that my faith could not keep us together. I felt that I'd failed everybody as a wife, a mother and a follower of Christ. This was the first Thanksgiving since the accident. Most of the rest of the world had carried on. By now our tragedy was just a small blip in the history of someone else's life. I knew we would soon have to let Kristen know the situation. It was a burden I could not carry.

From my journal, Thanksgiving weekend of 2005:

*** *Sunday, Fehr's are having their thanksgiving dinner, but Sat night K&K came over and a friend of theirs called to ask if Kev wanted two Bomber game tickets for Sun afternoon. So* *we decided Ralph & Kev would go to the football game, lucky them. After the family thanksgiving dinner Kristen and I left about 3pm and came home. I had a half hour nap and then we went off to Morden Lake and Golf course to go walking. The fresh air and crisp fall leaves with their changing colors made for an invigorating walk. After about an hour and a half I told Kristen about Ralph — that in order to give him space, he had this opportunity thru work of a different place, and so till the end of Oct he would be living there. "We are not separated," I said; "he would've liked to have gone trucking, but this is what he is doing instead." I tried to make it as positive as I could. She was just quiet and crying. Wow I have been nothing but the bearer of bad news for her, it seems. She expressed sadness, anger and amazement that I took it in stride so well. I told her "Kristen, I will not be able to nag him into coming back. God does not want our marriage to come apart."*

Kristen said, "I know we lost Jordan and Brittany, but DON'T I COUNT FOR ANYTHING?? I feel as if he doesn't even care about me."

Ralph informed Kevin on the way to Winnipeg. So when they got home, all of us talked for a little bit. Kristen did go over to give her dad a hug. He told her he loved her very much. Ralph — we all need you — I pray to God that you can get over this part of it and get back in the game where you belong. Boy I'm starting to get very tired and sleepy. This whole business is so taxing and draining. ***

That same evening, Kristen and I had stopped to watch the sunset from the edge of the golf course with the lake shimmering to our left. It was a beautiful sight and a reminder that there is still much beauty left in this world. I distinctly remember sharing with Kristen that, "Never in all my life had

I experienced to such an extent the heaviness and brokenness of the fall, the effects of sin and death on this world." We prayed together, and as we turned east to head back home, just above the horizon like a giant globe suspended in the air hung the most stunning Harvest Moon I had ever seen. We gazed at its beauty in silence, sensing for ourselves the reminder of God's promise that even though the light of day may go, when you experience the darkness of the night, He will send a light for you.

A Walk through the sculpture garden

The Winnipeg Assiniboine Park has the Leo Mol sculpture garden set in the English Gardens. This place has special memories for me. The last mother and daughter time I had with Kristen, Brittany and myself included a picnic and time to meander through the gorgeous grounds. We have some fun pictures of Kristen and Brittany climbing on the statue of *The Blower*, a tall replica of a man in 18th century garb blowing into a huge trumpet. Had I known this was the last mother and daughter time with all three of us, I would have memorized every detail in my mind or in my journal. The photographs convey the sense of joy, freedom and love as we delighted in each other's company. We took a picture under a twisted weathered old tree, surrounded by beautiful impatiens flowers in shades of pink and white. We are all smiling—*Life is Good* the picture says. This garden became a haven for me ... I would travel there for a place to contemplate amidst the beauty.

From my journal, Oct 14, 2005:

*** *Dear Britt*

I'm sitting here beside the pond in the Leo Mol sculpture garden. This and the English Gardens—I think of them as our spot. I miss you so much, the hole is just so big. But today I smile as I walk through here—remembering being here with you— remembering your beautiful smile—your love of flowers and your love of the lily pads. Britt—there is no sign that says 'Do not pick the lily pad flowers'—so I picked one for you. Nearly uprooted the whole plant. And the smile I have as I've walked through is because I've already decided, I'm picking a bouquet for you, to bring to the cemetery—I know you're not there. But I feel a connection with you more here than there, I just wanted to pick you some flowers from our favorite flower garden—I bet you have seen far more beautiful ones in heaven and I hope you're saying "I can hardly wait to show these to my mom," cuz Britt I can hardly wait till I can see them with you. Reminds me of us taking the Rock from Lake Louise, sneaking it under our jackets, there also was no sign that said "Do not pick the rocks." Kristen has gotten into 'the rock thing'. Do you know that she brought me a rock from the top of Mt Sinai—amazing. In eternity I'm hoping all of these struggles will be so distant.

I just wanted to tell you today how special a daughter you are and have been. I love you and will love you forever. Say hi and a huge hug to Jordan, and to Jamie. The world is just not as bright a place without your smiles, laughter, and songs.

All right, I'm going to go pick some flowers for you—Miss you.

Love you.... Mom ***

A SIDE TRIP AND A DOG NAMED CINDER

In November, on a spur of the moment decision, I booked a trip to see my sister in Portland, Oregon.

No, I know you cannot run away from your problems, but you can take a break from them.

Here we were, three women connecting on levels previously unknown. We were all going through our own valleys. My niece, had given birth three-and-a-half months previously to an adorable son, and was experiencing the challenges of single parenting, temporarily living with her mother, my sister. We discussed a whole range of emotionally charged topics, from our disappointments with God, the cycle of life, birth and death, to the powerful hungers of a nursing mother and the prospect of me getting a puppy. Unfortunately, my overwhelming sense of shame kept me from admitting that Ralph and I were struggling in our marriage. I probably admitted we had struggles, but I could not admit that he was not living with me.

I recall a moment with my sister, standing outside near her Magnolia tree, which would be stunning in spring. We were doing some fall gardening. She, dressed in shorts, gardening gloves and a cheery smile, suggested we dig in the dirt. I wanted to just blurt out, "Ralph is not living with me," but something kept me from saying it. It was as if keeping it a secret prevented it from being true. Just like 'the damn flowers' coming ... once people knew about your trauma it reinforced its reality. At that moment, I still had the hope that it was only for a short time. I knew she knew there was a problem, she just gave me a big hug. My sister has always respected people's need for privacy. I kept it to myself.

Later we sat on the balcony overlooking two levels of houses and green yards. How did she get this stunning view in the city, surrounded by trees, and the sound of birds calling from all directions. The sunniness of the day was broken by the sound of the phone ringing. No one got up to answer it until we heard Ralph's voice at the other end, telling me he was not sure he could make it in to Winnipeg to pick me up from the airport, because of a snow storm. How prophetic it felt ... at that moment I sat in the sunshine, on a deck enjoying breakfast, warmth and relationship, and all that waited for me in Manitoba seemed cold, icy and stormy.

I wished I could stay somewhere else forever.

The inability to let anyone know about Ralph's decision to move out of our home, kept me in a state of anxiety. I was horrified someone might find out. I couldn't cope with it, and I felt ashamed.

Shame is a horrible devastator.

THE DOG provided incentive that brought me back to Manitoba. Before I set out for Oregon, I had gone to look at puppies that were almost old enough to leave their mother, debating would I get a girl or a boy? Both had their positives and negatives. Supposedly female's personalities were just a bit gentler, so I had decided to go for the female dog. After my short Portland trip, Kristen came with me to make the final selection, and on that day, here was this cute little black guy with white paws and white chest spot. He looked at me, as if to say, "I'm the one for you." He captured my heart. I could hold him in the palm of one hand, such a tiny, squirmy little ball of mini black fluff. A wee whimper was the only sound he made and I wanted to take him home and snuggle him. All the prior intelligent decision-making went out the window, as I succumbed to his charm. Full of hope and enthusiasm, and a tiny bit of a doubt as to what I was thinking, I took him home with me.

I felt a slight sense of guilt because both Jordan and Britt had wanted a dog and never had the opportunity to have one. Having grown up on the farm, Ralph felt that dogs were for the outdoors and not meant to be in town, so he had overruled any petitions for dogs that came up. I hadn't been convinced myself, that we could handle a dog back then, although we did have turtles, guinea pigs, rabbits and fish. I offered an apology to my children about not having pushed harder for them to have had a dog when they were younger. About age ten, Britt said to me, "One day I'm going to live in the country and have horses, dogs, cats (she might have thrown in sheep) and all kinds of animals," to which I replied "that will be so good, and I will love to come and visit you there."

So now what should I name the puppy? At the time I was reading the book, *The Sacred Romance* by Brent Curtis and John Eldredge. The authors had expressed our human desire to live a fairytale-like story, the Cinderella story, where the prince comes and rescues the heroine. They compared God to the only one who could provide a 'happy-ever-after' scenario; as God was in the business of eternity. Those had been some of my thoughts, along with name contemplation as I went to sleep. In the middle of the night, the word Cinder came to mind. Waking up that morning, I knew it was a word of significance. Taking out my trusty old Webster dictionary, I looked up the definition of cinder and trembled as I read, *"Having been met with fire but not reduced to ashes."*

I knew I had been given a perfect name for the dog and confirmation of the decision. It was also reflective or short for Cinderella, the desire for a happy-ever-after life. I took Cinder home, sometimes I called him Cinder-fella, since he was a male. He brought a lot of joy and made a significant dent in the void of loneliness. He was tiny, loveable and huggable! A real heart throb. Ralph joked once, "if you get a dog I won't ever need to come back." Since he wasn't showing signs of returning just yet, it wasn't an issue. Cinder was good for all of us.

CHAPTER TEN

A GRIEF DECEMBERED

Moving on to Christmas

The dreading of Christmas began in April of that first year. I started to voice that concern in June, after my trip to Africa. With all the dramas and pressures of the summer, the failed expectation of what should have been, the angst of Christmas remained a silent black cloud waiting for its own time to bring about the storm.

As my sister said, I'd always been the "Queen of Christmas." I truly loved that festive time of year, the fresh snowfall, the fragrant tree, and the gatherings of loved ones; our own little Fehr family traditions of painting ornaments, playing the Carol game in which two teams battle to come up with the first line of a Christmas song, until someone runs out of lines. No repeats were allowed—unless it was the same song in a different language, that was the exception to the rule. We had hot apple cider in Christmas mugs and mandarin oranges after the tree was set up, along with chocolate mallow and cherry oatmeal cookies. The stockings were hung by the mantle with care to be opened Christmas day in the evening. Ralph led the ritualistic setting-up of the carefully chosen real tree. He would set it up in the stand, after having re-sawn the end to make it smooth. Next a plastic disc was nailed into the bottom and we would apply the twist-like retaining screws from three sides until the tree would stand proud and erect waiting for decorations, and then Ralph would leave. He reminded me of my father at that point, who felt that decorating needed to be done more perfectly. Ralph could run out of patience with little hands that would mess up the tree, so we learned early in the lives of our family, that it was best if he set up the tree properly, helped distribute the lights evenly and that was all. He would go entertain himself with his work while we revelled in putting up the decorations. He would join us for the traditional after decorating snack and tree admiration time. An evening was spent hand-painting an ornament that would adorn the tree, alongside a new ornament that I would buy for each of them every year. The progression of artistry with the ornaments conveyed the story of children growing up.

"When you leave home you can each take your ornaments with you and have a start for your own family traditional tree," I would tell them. Someday I thought I might have a designer tree, although it never appealed to me—truly I loved the eclectic assortment of ornaments, so rich with history and memories. Now they taunted me in the basement. Especially poignant were the new little white angels, I had bought in the after Christmas sales/January 05, with their names. I had purchased one for Jamie as well, as this year she was to be a part of the expanded family traditions. The tears flowed as I unpacked their named angels, knowing that by now they had met up with heavenly angels. Everyone gets nostalgic at Christmas time.

I became obsessed with the idea of going away at Christmas ... something I'd never wanted to do before. I always loved being around the extended family and friends. Everyone wears a special scarf of kindness that seems to ward off the coldness of the other eleven months of the year. Come December everyone is smiling, laughing, being kind and friendly. As a nurse, I'd read articles saying that many elderly and sick people had staved off their deaths until after Christmas. There is a hope and a reason for people to give a bit more and celebrate at this season.

And I loved to celebrate. I loved the traditions. But almost everything around traditions involves the people you love most dearly. Previously in talking to other women who had married children, we discussed how we would have to adjust to share our kids with the other sides of families. *Oh my goodness, how feeble, I now thought. At least you have your kids on the planet.*

I had to say and realize, "*I will never celebrate Christmas ever again with everyone in my family.*" Our last Christmas all together as a family had been three years before, in 2002, but we had had no idea it would be our last. We knew that we would probably spend the season apart as time went on, especially given Kristen and Kevin's desire to live and work in African countries. Now I had to face the harsh, cruel fact that on this earth I *would never again* have my family "Home for Christmas." "All Hearts come home for Christmas".... BAH HUMBUG! I wanted to yell and scream, weep and wail. I knew I needed to be away for this first Christmas.

The foreboding mounted along with other difficulties.

I broached the idea of going away, with Ralph, Kristen and Kevin. With some initial hesitation and concern, they all agreed. Kevin's folks were gracious enough to offer their blessing on our decision to leave. While someone else asked me, "Do you think it will help to run away?" What did they think *would* help? The only thing I could think of was to leave; I could not face Christmas in my hometown.

A retreat centre in Florida offered free accommodation for wearied workers to rejuvenate. Because Kristen and Kevin qualified technically, after filling out various papers providing appropriate supporting evidence, the centre accepted our application. We were able to plan a different Christmas, one of which I knew there would be too many.

It gave me something to almost look forward to, in facing the daunting task of learning 'to do Christmas' without Jordan and Brittany. My sister from the states and her daughters were coming out, I would not normally leave in that case but *there was nothing normal* in my life. My family was very understanding and supportive.

At least we would be away, in different circumstances. I envisioned a possibility to celebrate the real reason for the season, to have the focus on God's love. We purchased the tickets and I was able to put the dread of December on the back burner for a while.

A reverie from my Journal:

*** *In her mind she goes back and revisits Christmases past, whether they are memories, or photographs in her sub-conscious she is uncertain, as her life now seems to play in front of her. She is unsure as to whether she is a participant in it, or viewing her story from an anaesthetized distance, removed from the incredible sorrow.*

The first Christmas with a baby at her breast, she reflected on Mary the mother of Jesus and wondered how Mary must have felt as she held the promise and hope of the world in her arms. How she must have loved that baby with all her heart, the innocence of those eyes gazing up at her while gently nursing.

An eternal soul within those baby eyes, and then the baby burps, spits up, fusses a bit and with a few more sucks will drift into a peaceful sleep. And just as Mary had, she embraces the baby securely in her arms, knowing that for the moment all is right in the world, wishing she could stave off the inevitable pain that was to come.

There is the Christmas picture of her two-year-old daughter as she stands in holy awe by the tree, entranced by the glimmering lights that sparkle, reflected in her wide open eyes.

Somewhere in the mix of family focused celebrations, they begin to include a sister and her family for Christmas mornings. It is a joyful time of extra people in the household, and the beginning of the 'Fehr family Christmas sleepover.' Since the basement is transformed into the holiday get away including hot tub, the three siblings started their own tradition of a sleepover on the floor on Christmas Eve. The new tradition is that Jordan would get sick, as he once had, due to anxiety or over indulgence on sweets at grandma Krahn's. They never knew the cause, but the legend lived on long after the nausea passed, and jokingly he is reminded about that each year. Even when Kevin joined the family, it remained important to Kristen that they all sleep on the floor for the night. Kevin endured the initiation night; he and Jordan began forming a brotherly bond that unfortunately was cut short. The tunes of "Christmas Time in the Cabbage Patch" with the rooster heralding the dawn, become the morning announcement that 8 am had arrived, and it was time to open the presents. She laughs as she wonders how they managed to keep the eager children in bed until 8 am all those mornings. Even stranger was that in their teen years they resisted the desire to sleep for another few hours, and still responded to the Cabbage Patch bugle call.

She flashes forward to more recent times. The first year that Kristen and Kevin were in Africa, there is a picture of Ralph, Jocelyn, Jordan and Brittany looking somewhat sad with extra plates set for 'the Africans.' Another picture is taken as they were toasted in Kenya, and toasted for their future return, and for the next year when they would all be together. The most recent year, 2004, included Jamie and a new tradition that would hopefully carry on ... a chocolate fondue on the 25th in the evening. They'd already realized someone was going to be in conflict because Jamie's family also celebrated on Christmas Eve. She had wondered how the traditions would have to alter. Wistfully she now wished that those would be the only concerns of the season ... how to alternate and juggle everyone's schedules so it could be made to work that the family could be together somewhere during this time.

She had even written herself a note that had been placed with the decorations, as she'd packed them away the last year they'd been together. It said, "Joc don't be sad as you get out the decorations knowing that K&K are not here at Christmas ... There is so much to be thankful for." That note only brought her more tears.

She realized that since 1980, she has marked off her life according to the episodes of her children, the momentous events and the daily ones. All of life seemed focused on the children. Events cloud in her mind, and she is not sure if it was when Jordan was this age or was it Brittany?

Now her life was no longer marked by the years the kids did this or that; there was one big mark, life before and life after The Accident. She knew this would always be the marking on her soul. But she determined it would not be the last mark. She clung to the hope that there would be joy again somewhere in the Christmases to come.

She was jolted back to the reality of Christmas 2005... the first Christmas after the accident. Her daughter had thoughtfully given her a book on grieving the holidays, "A Decembered Grief" by Harold Ivan Smith, with practical tips from people who had lost family members and how to do the holidays without them. Some very feasible suggestions, some very painful ones, were included. She does not even open many of the Christmas cards. She glanced at the envelopes and if she suspected it was just a picture of a smiling family, she tossed it. She realized that people had no idea how painful it was to receive family picture cards. The picture said, "Look at how big our family is, look at how happy we are." The only thing it said to her, "You have lost much." ***

December 22 was the departure date for Florida, and what would be a very different Christmas—at this point I did not know how very different.

From my journal:

*** December 18, 2005

Christmas has long been my favourite time of the year. This year is so unbelievable. I still feel like I'm watching a movie of someone's life—but then to see the plot—what a tragic story and against anything I can do, I've been cast as the main character of this unbelievable tragedy. It is not enough that her two children died, but her husband has abandoned her.

I had so much hope to keep me going. It is right for our marriage to work out. But my hope is fading. I am beginning to despair.

> *Oh come let us adore Him......*
> *Risen with healing in His wings*
> *Mild He lays His glory by*
> *Born that man no more may die.*

Born to raise the sons of earth, born to give them second birth.

These words have become so true for Jord & Britt...but the pain of us left behind. The curse of the earth is death, this has been so prevalent in my thoughts and what Jesus brought is eternal life.

Remind me again Lord—that we have hope in you.
Jesus be my vision—this pain feels too much to bear.

Lord you keep reminding me that I have to forgive—and it feels like Ralph keeps doing things that require forgiveness.

PLEASE LORD, intervene in our lives. "Ask me anything in my name and I will do it." Jesus you said it-please do it! I can ask in boldness for our marriage to survive, because you have ordained marriage.

Pastor Herb spoke about Heaven today. Thank you Lord for bringing it home again. Help me to live in light of eternity.

May the words of my mouth and the meditations of my heart be pleasing in your sight, O Lord, my rock and my redeemer. (Ps 19:14 NIV)

He has showed you, O man, what is good. And what does the Lord require of you? To act justly and to love mercy and to walk humbly with your God. (Micah 6:8 NIV)

OK I keep wanting to point out things for Ralph, in all my readings, etc.—ways to point out to him, how disobedient he is to walk away from his marriage vows and his family. But I am to love mercy, even when he walks away from me, God loves him and will forgive him. I have forgiven him a lot, but it feels like I have a limit and Lord it feels like he's getting mighty close to the limit. ***

Tuesday night: *wow*, I had planned to have supper with Ralph, but he called and said he was going to Winnipeg for a hockey game. Earlier, he had declined the option to go. I was a bit upset, but alright; I called later and left a message on his cell, that I hoped he'd have a good time. My friend Dorothy called, and we decided to go see the movie, *The Lion Witch and the Wardrobe*. It was great. We had tea at her house after. One line from the movie particularly affected me: after Edmund had betrayed his siblings and went to the white witch, Aslan forgave him, even though the community labelled him a traitor. Aslan told the siblings, *what is done is done and we need speak of it no more*. He, Aslan, granted Edmund forgiveness and mercy, that struck me. I told Dor I was reminded of having to forgive—but not expecting I'd need to put it into practise immediately.

From my journal:

*** *Dec 20th The darkest hour comes just before the dawn, well the hour of my soul is very dark. Hear our plea oh Lord—please intervene in our situation.*

Lord please purify me—I am not trying to do this for me, I really felt this would be best for all of us. Ralph asked me yesterday on the way home from a medical procedure, for which I'd been sedated (which was done I believe because of the physical symptoms of stress on my system) ... He asked me "How bad would it be if I didn't come to Florida for Christmas?"

Oh Lord, where do I go with this?

Oh Lord—he feels you are far removed from him. Please step down.

Light of the world—you stepped down into darkness, open my eyes, let me see. (Words of a song.)

You are my sustainer and my strength, I was hoping we could get away from all this intensity. His mind is certainly not functioning normally as Rita said. She is a psych nurse and has dealt with anxiety disorders, there are those caused by post-traumatic stress syndrome, which is what Ralph had been diagnosed with. As Rita said, 'All our way of relating and how we had done things has totally changed, all the rules have changed.'

I don't want to make Kristen choose between her mom and dad, so do we all stay home?

WHAT DO WE DO??? ***

(The writing in my journal gets bigger as the intensity comes out in the pen through the next few questions.)
*** Oh Lord—Kristen has lost her brother and sister—I have lost my son & daughter—are we to lose our father and husband???

Oh-God—Please, Please

Can you help us? This is so huge, because it represents SO MUCH! ***

To me this felt like the end of my marriage.

Still from my journal:

*** Jordan & Brittany dying was unbearable, but this on top of all that—and from the man I'd committed my life to, for him to say no felt like the death blow to the marriage.

I don't know at what point exactly I was in the family room listening to music and I just realized technically everything was taken away from me—any resources I'd relied on during life. I felt stripped bare—it was God and I—and I would hang onto Him.

I wailed and moaned, oh how I've moaned and groaned. Lord, I knew that I had to decide that I had to still trust in you,

YOU ARE REAL — You have to be!
There was a tiny spark of peace.
Though all else be taken away from me — my husband, two of my children.
Kristen would be devastated at this point, I did not have a lot of hope for my marriage, but I already knew that God would have me forgive Ralph and also try to understand that the usual Ralph would not do this to us. "But Lord you need to intervene in his life too" — now was not the time to bargain or say I will trust you if you give me back Ralph.
The question to me was simply, "Will you trust me?"
"And Lord, all I have is that you will be with me? Each time it feels like you ask more and more."
At that moment there was nothing left.
I have no control. ***

From my journal, December 23, 10:56 pm

*** Well here I am in Florida, and Ralph is not.

This is the first Christmas I think in 32 years that we will not spend time together. How bizarre.

By the blood of Jesus Christ, I declare victory for the soul of Ralph.

Lord I pray for victory in our marriage.

It would be easier to go through this if I knew the outcome would be good. But that is where faith has to step in. These are words people hear and say, but to actually be living this drama is unbelievable.

We believe Lord — Help my unbelief. ***

From my journal, December 24, Christmas Eve in Florida:

*** *Thank you Lord, on this Xmas eve on a balcony in Florida, watching you paint the skies with beauty—may you paint my life with your beauty. Bless our Christmas Lord. I am glad we are here instead of Winkler. All the usual trappings of Xmas are gone—snow, gatherings, decorations, etc,etc. It really is you & me Lord—and that will be enough. No, it is not just you & me ... K&K are here also. Thank you.* ***

We had what you would call a God moment on Christmas Eve. Earlier in the day, we rode the open air tourist bus up and down Anna Marie Island, trying to decide where to go for Christmas Eve. The church that appealed to us the most was one that listed a candlelight service for 8 pm (that's what we read). After a fairly light supper, we hurried to the church and were surprised to find very few people there, basically no one. Flickering candles in pails lit the walkway to the church, but the sanctuary was deserted. Oh shoot, we thought, it was going to be one of those awkward nights where only about ten people show up, and you stick out like a sore thumb! But as we walked into the back of the church, a man approached us. We said we were here for the service. "Did you know that it started at nine?" Sections of the music were going to be rehearsed before the actual event. The three of us wondered what to do; should we walk and wait until nine? We were sure we had read 8 pm on the poster board. For the time being, we decided to sit in the back pews and catch our breath.

Within minutes, the soloist began with a song sung by Mary, the mother of Jesus, as she is heading toward Bethlehem, some of the words:

I have travelled many moonless nights
Cold and weary, with a babe inside
Holy Father, you have come
Chosen me now, to carry your son
　　I am waiting in a silent prayer

I am frightened by the load I bear
In a world as cold as stone
Must I walk this path alone?
Be with me now, be with me now
Breath of Heaven, hold me together, be forever near me ...
breath of Heaven
Breath of Heaven, lighten my darkness
Pour over me Your Holiness ... for You are Holy.
Help me be strong .... be forever near me, Breath
of Heaven.

(Original words by Chris Eaton, sung by Amy Grant)

The three of us sat in stunned silence at the end of the song, silence perhaps broken by the sound of tears dropping to the floor. For Kristen, this had been her song of the season; she had brought a CD version of it to share with me on Christmas day. And now we had been blessed with a private rendition of a very powerful song. We left the sanctuary in silence, headed towards the pier, and passed the time until the official service at 9 pm. Although the real service had already happened for us!! After all wasn't Christmas /Emmanuel all about the presence of God in a broken and weary world?

Extremely weary and broken, we had just been given the gift of HOPE.

The *Daily Bread* devotional reading for that Dec. 24 also delivered encouragement.

In the author's reflections on Mary, he states:

She abandoned herself to God's will in the present and received the grace to do what God asked of her. What is God asking you to do? It may be something magnificent or something ordinary. It may be to respond actively to a command in scripture, or to submit patiently to present suffering.

(David Roper TDB, Dec 24 2005)

"What God arranges for us to experience at each moment is the holiest thing that could happen to us," according to 18th century writer Jean-Pierre de Caussade.

"Are you able to accept each moment with grace and submission?" was the final and difficult question of the reading.

From my journal:

*** *Christmas Day 2005*
WOW—Here I sit, on a beach watching powerful waves roll in. The last two days, the water has been calm, but there is power here! And I do have HOPE.

Yet each time I get a sense of hope—I am afraid, because each time I've had hope or expressed it—it seems to have been dashed, and another worse scenario has arisen.

I think last Wed morning was the lowest point in my life. It felt as though I had lost all, and what is left? Not much except you & I God.

For just a little while now, I want to bask in the sunshine and sense the power you have God.

*Give me strength to face what lies ahead, because I'm not going back to anything easy. ***

CHAPTER ELEVEN

A WEARY NEW YEAR 2006

January first arrived with lacklustre hope. The customary sense of anticipation and new resolve was missing; at least the old year was over and I did not think any year could match 2005 in difficulty. How wrong I could be. The new year arrived with the cumulative effect of all that had gone on in 2005. January was usually my worst month and this January did not disappoint. It carried the dread of the one-year anniversary of the accident looming ahead and our marriage falling behind. I contemplated seeking a counsellor, something I was okay with trying but unsure of where to go. Even the search process seemed too much for me. There was no doubt I had serious difficulty in coping with my life circumstances. I also did not want people to know what was going on in our lives. To live in a small town had its good moments, especially the support we received after the accident, but now the pressure mounted as people wanted to know "How are Ralph and Joc doing?" It became too much for me. I felt the need to hide out. Too often prayer chains and gossip lines cross boundaries.

In addition the emotional roller coaster of Ralph's increased anxiety issues was taking its toll on all of us. Men and women handle grief and stress differently, and each individual's response is unique.

At the time of the accident people said, "You will never be the same." Of course we recognized that. And yet, now that we were so different, so affected by our tragedy, people seemed surprised.

This was a very strange situation.

The reality is that many of us imagine what things would be like *if* such and such should happen. In these hypothetical situations, we know we would grieve. We feel pseudo-pain in our minds, but then because it is not an actual scenario in our lives, because we only *imagine* our response, we move on to the next hypothetical situation. Because these academic responses are based on making decisions in a healthy state of mind, a mind that only speculates about the loss of a child, or speculates about a marriage break-up, and not a mind drowning in sorrow, there is little connection between how we *think* we might respond and what actually happens. In reality, after months of being exhausted by emotional trauma and strain, nerves are frayed, love and commitment are seriously challenged; this became my hellish *new reality.*

Control is an illusion, yet we all strive to maintain some control of something, however small. When my life began to spiral out of control and it appeared normal all around me, an internal battle developed between knowing how to cope and where I could turn to for professional help and support.

Our home church had been extremely supportive in our early grief process. Unfortunately people who struggle in their marriages experience a lot of shame. The church has been slow to face the issues of divorce, also of homosexuality and depression, but forced to, in light of them showing up in the congregation. Ralph and I sensed a turning point in support and understanding once people found out we had marriage problems. They did not know what to say to us. It increased the anxiety for us by trying to keep our separation from being known. We did not feel like we wanted to be more gossip fodder. We were trying to work things out. Ralph and I shared suppers and talked most days. But, it felt as though we had disappointed everyone in our lives, by not coping in our marriage.

We began attending a church in the neighbouring community.

"When shame denies me a place in Your fold, In Your Love remember me."

Steve Bell song *Remember Me* from the psalms.

The dictionary defines shame in the following way.

shame | sh ām|

noun

• a painful feeling of humiliation or distress caused by the consciousness of wrong or foolish behavior

• a loss of respect or esteem; dishonor

• used to reprove someone for something of which they should be ashamed

• [in sing.] a regrettable or unfortunate situation or action

• a person, action, or situation that brings a loss of respect or honor

What a shame that shame itself is so debilitating.

Within a week of Feb. 27, 2005 we had moved from being a family respected in the community to the family that everyone was glad they were not.

As if that was not bad enough, when the stress crumbled the foundations of our marriage, we added shame to our load of heartache and sorrow. This was probably one of the most painful aspects for me, within the church community—that we felt shame for our marriage difficulties. People who are struggling cannot cope with judgemental attitudes. This is certainly one area in which the church could take some lessons from secular society. In many other circles people thought it was not surprising to be separated or divorced. I didn't agree with the casual approach to marriage, but in a different community, I never felt the stigma of shame or humiliation for the condition of my marriage. Living in one of the Bible belts has definite advantages; however, in trying circumstances the judgemental attitude of some communities can cause further wounding.

With your own judgements you are judged. I found this to be true. I knew I had previously had little experience, empathy or understanding for those who had divorced. Marriages were designated by God, and it was very clear in the Bible that *God hates divorce.* I knew it, our church knew it, and our discussions on the topic were very short. There was little to say. Divorce was viewed as wrong, end of story.

After my marriage trials, I apologized numerous times to a sister who had been divorced earlier. I simply said, "I am so sorry, for having had such a poor understanding of your situation and for my lack of support." I am sure I never stated any condemnation—but in my self-righteous ways, my judgement would have unlovingly oozed out of my pores. Even when disapproval was not verbalized, the recipients sensed it very quickly, as I began to experience.

There were a couple of ladies that spoke to me, ones who had lost a child. One lady in particular called to say, if I wanted to talk, please please let her know. She knew how difficult the loss of a child was on their marriage. Only by God's grace had they survived.

I wanted to call her. I hoped God's grace was going to be sufficient for me, for us. But it was my shame and embarrassment that probably kept me from making that call. Voicing the fears, saying it aloud also acknowledged that there was a problem. Not that I didn't admit that there was one. I was tired of people wanting to know about me, about my life. My sense of privacy felt invaded. This part of the journey was what spurred me on to get professional help. In that safe space I could pour out my heart. Probably God and Todd heard my most ardent cries.

Shame and guilt must be among the most debilitating tools of the devil. Shame keeps people from moving on with their lives, although the shame is often perceived more in the eye of the afflicted, than it really is. People feel ashamed for not having the strength and ability to cope with situations beyond themselves.

The verses that offered encouragement to me came from the Psalms:

Those who look to Him are radiant; their faces are never covered with shame. Psalm 34:5 NIV

> *To you, Oh Lord, I lift up my soul;*
> *in you I trust, oh my God.*
> *Do not let me be put to shame,*
> *nor let my enemies triumph over me.*
> *NO ONE WHOSE HOPE IS IN YOU*
> *WILL EVER BE PUT TO SHAME, ...*
> *REMEMBER, OH LORD, YOUR GREAT MERCY AND LOVE, Psalm 25:1-3, 6 NIV emphasis mine*

After a particularly difficult week, I found this note on my door.

Dear Joc

I am sorry to hurt you so much and so constantly. I so want to be your friend during this time when I am not really being your husband. I am sorry I am in such a state of mental melt down. Most days I have at least some hope. You have been the strongest person ever through this ... I know you have God giving you strength. Thank you Joc, for being my strongest supporter through this to date.

I do love you. Ralph

January also brought about Kristen and Kevin's move to Alberta, two provinces over, in order for both of them to attend school. They were taking courses to facilitate their desire for full time international work. In some ways, this was good for both of us. I felt a little less pressure for trying to pretend things were better than they were with Ralph and I; but I knew I would miss my daughter enormously.

After her move to Alberta, Kristen began to see a counsellor. At this point, a major issue for her was the situation with her parent's marriage. In absentia, this counsellor diagnosed Ralph with delayed grief process. I was sure there was a lot of merit to his conclusion. The legitimate questions this diagnosis raised, however is were, "What was the grief process?" "How do you do it?" "Was there a given time frame?" We are all individuals with different coping mechanisms, different triggers, and different responses. The ultimate challenge remains: how to carry on in life, still recognizing that the horrible loss does affect your being, mind, body and soul. Pain and suffering make it difficult to to focus on anything beyond that pain and suffering. I was a surgical nurse, if someone came for treatment with us; it could be surgically removed, requiring a healing time of 6-8 weeks, or 3-5 months for major surgery. Grief, however, was more like a cancer that ate away at your heart and soul; you never knew what area it would assault next. As in medicine, the chemotherapy and radiation treatments for this sickness are less precise and definitive in their effectiveness. My heart ached for Ralph;

his ongoing panic attacks and ineffective treatment plans robbed him of both his strength, and his desire to fight.

My prayer: *Lord, you are the healer.*

Could you come down to bring your healing into our lives?

Conflicting advice came to me from many places and in many ways:

"If that were my husband, I'd just tell him to move back home."

"Don't expect anything from him; continue to give him his space."

"Is he taking anything?"

"Keep praying, God wants your marriage to be healed."

"Have you done marriage counselling?"

I had made an appointment for counselling, but it would have to wait until February.

On many a day, it was a challenge just to get myself out of bed. Work at the hospital helped me to function a few days a week, but the winter driving to get there was horrible for me. When people at work would talk about the weather and poor road conditions. My mind trilled "la de da de da....." trying to block out the images of my children's car skidding on icy roads. Reports of accidents that had happened due to ice caused further anxiety. At the end of the workday I often wondered how I had managed to make it through my shift.

One blustery January morning, we had an emergency added to our surgery list. It was a young man—born the same year as my son Jordan—whose car had slid out of control and collided with oncoming traffic. He claimed he, "was lucky to be alive" and his anxious wife was so relieved. I couldn't cope. I asked one of the other nurses if she could relieve me in that room for a while as I went to regroup. Why had my son not been lucky like that, suffering only a broken leg?

My co-workers were extremely kind and understanding, but we still needed to function as a professional surgical team. I faced many other challenges at work, but overall it still brought more satisfaction than staying home. Sadly, there was no place that was challenge free and very few sanctuaries of peace and freedom.

Nature was a solace.

From my journal:

*** *Beautiful fresh snow yesterday and more today.*

SNOW ANGELS

> *I made three angels in the snow yesterday*
> *I wondered how long their wings would stay.*
> *Today I passed that way again*
> > *Fresh snow softened the lines*
> > *Their mark still there,*
> *But angels belong in Heaven.*

> > *Jan 17-06 ***

January brought a battle with despair and depression, but I was reminded of God's caring. Three times in one week friends stopped by to bring flowers. Oh, I was blessed to have such a great support network around me. The biggest surprise blessing that cold January came on a Sunday morning with a phone call from an old high school friend. We had not spoken much over the years.

From my journal:

*** *She said to me, "Joc I want you to know you have been on my heart. I have been wanting to call you at various times, but this last time the sense was so persistent I couldn't resist it, but I said to God I have nothing to say to her, but He said, "I DO. I want her to know ... you are not forgotten."*

She quoted some verses about our mourning being turned to ashes. The picture she had in her mind as she'd been praying, was of us in a very dark place, but we were to be reminded that we were not forgotten. Also, she sensed God's presence reaching down into the darkness and lighting it up. Thank you Lord. I had tears streaming down my face as she shared this with me. Ralph was moved to tears as well. In church that morning, we sang one of my favourite songs, Alleluia, Grace like Rain falls down on me, alleluia all my (sins) stains are washed away, they're washed away. ***

In my new life, I had developed an odd connection with a Low German lady. Our town has a large low German population. Historically we have the same roots, but when the migrations of our ancestors took place, some conservative factions went to Mexico or South America, and other groups stayed in Canada. Culturally we had our differences, but this lady and I became connected through a grief experience. On a very cold evening in January, we met for coffee at the local Smitty's. Her marriage was also undergoing its share of difficulties, many of which had begun before their tragedy. This lady appeared meek and mild, but there was a strength, a feistiness evident. Over cups of steaming coffee she told me of her husband's controlling attitude. I thought I was 'older and wiser' in the ways of marriage relationships because I'd read numerous books, given the talks, so I asked her thoughtfully, "What attracted you to him in the first place?" (Marriage help 101, remind yourselves of what your husbands were like when you met, in the hope of recognizing that many of those qualities still exist.) Her answer in low German brought us into fits of laughter.

"Eck weit nicht, Schlapt eck?" Translated it meant, "I don't know; was I sleeping?"

Well, that was not the expected answer. What an interesting experience, sisters in the Lord, sharing our hurts about our husbands and life in general.

Then she asked me, again in low German, "Is it wrong to pray for your husband's death? Not a sudden death, a slow one?" *Goodness,* I thought, *did she want him to languish?*

"No, just so he would have time to make his peace with God." What a strange but sincere question. Death was one of the few options logistically open to a woman with her strict religious background. Divorce was not a viable choice, although she told me, she would leave if it were necessary.

At the end of the month, I flew to Edmonton with my sister-in-law Debbie to attend *Breakforth,* a spiritual praise and worship conference.

In some ways, eleven months later, the act of living had moved from a minute-to-minute existence to an hour-by-hour, or even day-to-day survival.

From my journal at the conference:

You Lord, are all I have and you give me all I need; my future is in your hands. I praise the Lord, because He guides me and in the night my conscience warns me. I am always aware of the Lord's presence; He is near, and nothing can shake me. Good News, Psalm 16:5,7,8

*** Sat Jan 28th Well Lord I have been shaken but I am aware of your presence. Lord breathe your life giving spirit into me and make your presence known. Thank you Lord for this time to 'come apart.' Yes in all senses, as I've said I'm a high needs, high maintenance case right now. Love you God! ***

I returned to Manitoba with some new inspiration, but also with the dread of facing the one-year anniversary. The year had taken a huge toll on the small remnant of our family. And it appeared our family was getting smaller.

Technically I still had holiday time left, so I booked a week away in February, to return to Florida for the week over my birthday.

From my journal:

*** I asked Ralph if he wanted to come to Florida with me. What possessed me to ask him? That would be a dream come true, if he would decide to join me. Ha ha. Shouldn't even entertain thoughts like that, he can hardly spend 6 hours with me. Anyways last evening we had a teary time. We were both grieving Britt & Jord & Jamie.

I am so tired of my kids being dead.

C.S, Lewis said "Not only do we live each day in grief, we live each day thinking about living in grief."

The intensity is exhausting.

Also a blessing, Ralph got me a cell phone for my travels. I want to talk to him already. ***

CHAPTER TWELVE

POLKA DOTS OF HOPE
AND JOY IN THE
FABRIC OF SORROW

The days in my journal read as a tragedy interspersed with moments of sunshine and song.

Early on, I decided to trust God; then I had to decide each day, after day, that I would continue to trust.

My default mode *had* to be trust. Without that I would sink.

When it's dark and it's cold and I can't feel my soul ... you are so good,

When the world has gone grey and the rain's here to stay, you are still good ...

With every breath I take in, I'll tell you I'm grateful again

And the storm may swell and even then, it is well, and you are good.

Words from Song *You are Good* sung by Nicole Nordeman .

From my journal: Feb 16th 2006

*** *(I was in Florida again on my own for my birthday— well the dog was with me.)*

Today I choose to be thankful for who you are—for your presence with me—for the assurance that I will see my kids again. Thank you Lord for stretcher bearers, people who support us—a term used by Carol Kent in her book, Now I lay my Isaac Down.

Lord there is humour all around. One of the retirees was sitting around the pool. His cell phone rang and every one heard him say ... "I pressed the wrong damn button." I can relate to that. Two nights ago Ralph called; it was Valentine's Day. I was walking Cinder when the phone rang—Cinder lurched—I bumped my head on a tree branch & "I pressed the wrong damn button" and disconnected. He called back and it was good to talk to him. ***

Continuing from my journal a few days later:

*** Story of the Sand Dollar Shells. I think it was Monday I walked along the beach carrying Cinder. No dogs allowed on the beach. I am thinking in my head, partly talking "Lord remember the sand dollar shell I brought back from Florida at Christmas?" (These shells are circular with an intricate flower shaped design on the upper side; collectors go up and down the beach looking for intact shells.) Well, on the last visit, I had brought this one shell home after packing it carefully in my suitcase to survive travel. It had endured storms and been bashed up on the ocean shore—and Ralph picks it up in Winkler, and breaks it.

"Well maybe Lord, you could replace it?" I didn't even want to allow that thought to persist. I felt I was just setting myself up for disappointment ... but within a few minutes, there was a large sand dollar shell. (Take note I wrote last time we had difficulty finding some—Kevin had found one for me and I *found one.) "OK thank you Lord, it was as if you were giving me some HOPE"... then*

"Well Lord, maybe Ralph and I should each have one."

I am so much into the symbolism of things. Sure enough a few minutes later another one.

"What about one for K&K?"

"OK, how about one for each of them?"

"Why don't I just shut up now, but we've done so much thinking about things for J&B, how about an extra one for an extra blessing ... well if there was one more it would be one for each Jordan and Brittany."

"Well God, (now I felt like Lot arguing with God, if there are only 5 righteous people.) "Sorry Lord, we've done so many symbolic things—I'm sorry, I didn't even think of it, what about one for Jamie?"

I didn't really ask it aloud, I only thought it,

"I'm sorry to even think it."

Thank you Lord, you have blessed me with finding seven sand dollar shells in about 20 minutes—certainly unheard of in my previous experience! Thank you Lord—You are a God of detail. Not only that, but look at the detail of the shell, it is absolutely intricate and beautiful. Lord you are good!!

Thank you for this time of sonshine on my soul. ***

There were times God was so present and catered to my silly nostalgic emotional moments. And then I wondered, *God, if you could get so involved in such little things ... **WHY,** why couldn't you have done THE BIG THING and kept them* *alive?* That question did not seem to have a reply. The only answer that came, "I will be enough."

From my journal:

*** *Friday Feb 17. Had a dream last night and was awake quite a bit, maybe I should take a sleeping pill tonight—as Dr Reedyck says, "You can't fight the devil at night." But yes, you can, with scripture and prayer, it does seem tougher though. It was as though I was writing the book of our story—The Accidental Christian, only the accident refers to our kids—strange how the mind lacks reasoning when semi-awake. My mind ran through the phone call from the hospital, to our desperate drive, to crumpling at the news. Oh that just relived all the pain and the agony, so fresh, even writing this now—OH GOD—I give it to you. Help me to live my life in the right balance of remembrance and not getting stuck in it. ***

From my journal, Reflections from the oceanside:

*** *Feb 19th*

The lines between heaven and earth are blurred; it is as though one is a continuum of the next. Looking out at the horizon that is what I saw—earth meets sky. Heaven and earth are really closer together than we've lived. Help me to be eternity-minded in all I do, Lord. Thank you for your beauty here. ***

The return trip from Florida did not end all that well.

This was the first time I had travelled on my own. Generally, travel is better when shared with people whom you want to be with. Navigating new roads in a rental car, trying to read traffic directions, and getting back to the airport with only a nauseated dog as my passenger proved to be a challenge.

From my journal:

*** *OK a few final comments on my return from Florida— the trip back to the airport was similar to Britt's 'pizza delivery from hell.'* ***

Britt had worked for a short time in Canmore delivering pizza, using her own standard clutch maroon Chevy Cavalier with balding tires. One night she was delivering a pizza, to a destination unsure. She knew the general area—one of steep slippery roads in the hilly end of town. Her description of her escapades, reversing down a steep incline, up a one-way the wrong way, carrying the pizza in hand the last block, and stumbling on the driveway while keeping the pizza upright, sent us all into fits of laughter. She was sure the loaded pizza was cold by the time it was delivered, but the customer at the receiving end must have recognized that she had been through a lot to deliver it, and with a big smile, handsomely tipped her five dollars. A situation funniest in her telling of the story.

Back to journal:

*** *My car rental from hell. I thought I left in plenty of time. I had been menstruating on and off that whole week, so I thought by Monday morning leaving it should have tapered down. WRONG—I was nearly hemorrhaging—Sunday night I bought another box of 20 tampons just to be sure, by Monday morning at 7:15 am I was at the Publix store trying to buy super tampons, they only opened at 7:30 so I drove on to the next one. Bought them—used the bathroom in the store, stayed there about 15 minutes as I dripped on the floor, all over the toilet—what a bloody mess! I was so frustrated with God. I hadn't bled like this for years. The return route to Tampa from Anna Marie Island was not clearly marked, there were two toll booths, I only remembered one. I stopped at another bathroom. There was construction at the airport and I could see the* *road I needed to take, but could not seem to get ON it. Finally returned the car, took the shuttle back to the airport, Cinder out to pee, and a few minutes to recoup, because I could see my gate marked upstairs. Forgot, there is another shuttle train to the actual gate, and then the long line through security ... grumble grumble... *** We just barely made it.*

We connected in Minneapolis, a spread out airport with many walkways. Cinder just added the icing to the cake of the day. I had him stand on a moving walkway as we navigated from one end of the airport to the other, he had been given minimal food, as he had thrown up in his little breathable, pet duffel bag carrier. Here in the middle of this moving walkway, he suddenly squatted and did his doggy business. AAAAGH! Fortunately I had a little doggy bag in my pocket, and quickly scooped up him and the poop just as we reached the end of the walkway. All this rushing only to be delayed. The plane taxied out as if to depart, followed by a announcement from the pilot about "some difficulty on the computer screen," requiring maintenance. "Our apologies folks," and we taxied back to the terminal. Not only did we wait in the plane for forty-five minutes while they checked out the computer screen, we then had to reload onto a different plane. I think the most disappointing part for me, was that in my busy-ness trying to settle Cinder under the seat ahead of me, I missed the apology announcement for the delay and the offer for free drinks!

From my journal:

*** The One-Year Mark

February 28, 2006

We just survived the one-year anniversary. I can't believe it's been a whole year. When the waves wash over, it feels like it was yesterday and yet it seems forever ago that I last saw Brittany, Jordan and Jamie. As Kristen said, "The longest short year ever." Each day of the past 365 has been incredibly intense. Kristen gave me some earrings from Morocco, a silver leaf style, symbolic for me turning over a new leaf. Is there still some life left in us to produce a new leaf?

ONLY WITH YOU DEAR GOD, ONLY WITH YOU!! ***

***TRUST

For a long time I wondered if I could actually trust you Lord. I thought I did before Feb 27, 2005, but after publicly declaring it, and then the accident, it left me reeling. But I also knew deep in my heart,

IF I LOSE YOU, GOD, I LOSE EVERYTHING.

THE BOTTOM LINE IS, YOU ARE ALL THAT REALLY MATTERS.

And even as I write it here, I know I will struggle with this again.

Brittany and Jordan, you are still so loved and so missed.

So what's it like up there? ***

DANGERS ON THE ROAD

Here it was a year later and the highway of life was still fraught with emotional roadblocks. The warning signs should have been out every day ... Caution: dangerous trucks entering. Note to self: get out of the way.

From my journal:

*** From an email to sister-in-law, Debbie:

I thought my day was going fine today—and then someone from stats and employment called me. I think I have done some surveys for them in the past. She made it sound government related and that I was obligated to answer. It was all going fine ... until she asked how many bedrooms in our house? Was it mortgaged? How many residents in the house? I answered two. She asked when did Jordan & Brittany move out? I said, "Please do not ask me anymore questions, my kids were killed in an accident," and I hung up. I sank to the floor in a heap of tears and moans. It took me 45 minutes to recover enough to go out for a walk. ***

I had learned to navigate this unwelcome road very carefully, always avoiding potential emotional situations. Even with all the guarding, at times I would get blindsided, and have to try my best to recover. People had no idea what little image, song or saying would bring back a vivid memory of a better day of my life prior to February 27, 2005. "Just when you thought it was safe to go out again."

Grief in the Mirror

> *You in the mirror, staring back at me*
> *Hollow eyes, clothed in grief*
> *Who asked you to come?*
> *And why do you stay so long?*
> *Maybe you thought it was time to pay me a visit?*
> *You've been all about, spreading your 'Joy'*
> *But I could have done quite fine without your coming*
> *You were not invited, now leave me alone.*
> *I want back what you took from me.*
> *And what?*
> *You bring flowers, as if to soften your visit?*
> *I don't want Damn Funeral flowers.*

CHAPTER THIRTEEN
DATING MY HUSBAND

From my journal:

*** *March 12, 2006*

I'm tired of being disappointed with Ralph.

I'm tired of being disappointed with how little our prayers seem to be doing.

I am discouraged today—I feel tired of crying by myself as I am doing right now.

I'm tired of the ache I have when I think about Jordan, Jamie and Britt.

I am tired of hearing about M & M's disappointments, the daily reports of more difficulties with their baby—God I wish You would DO SOMETHING!

I'm tired of being, "hard to be with."

People don't know what to say to me—can't I be frivolous?

I am tired of the emotional intensity, daily, hourly, being guarded with all conversations—always having another dialogue running on in my head.

LORD, I AM TIRED OF ALL OF THIS!!

So what do I do??? I don't know, Lord.

I know that I have to lean on you— You are all I have.

(And right now I'm sorry to say it doesn't feel like enough.)

GOD, bring me some HOPE—I feel like I've carried on such a long time with a carrot dangling in front of me—always being pulled ahead. I don't know if the carrot is going to cut it, Lord. I want some real joy and happiness in my life. I want my husband back.

Are we allowed to just walk out of each other's lives??

(Did I mention I am tired of playing solitaire?) ***

Ralph had gone to a Promise Keepers seminar—I had urged him to go, paid for it and booked it. Apparently, women all across the nation try to get their husbands to go to these events. Unlike their female counterparts, who flock to the women's retreats, men need to be persuaded to go. On the other hand, offer a man a business seminar with finances as a main topic; that is a different scenario.

After the conference Ralph recounted a story that had challenged him. This great big black guy was the youngest of three brothers. While his oldest brother was away at his third year of college on a football scholarship, he was killed in a car accident. This younger brother vividly remembered his dad being flown home from his out of town business trip, walking into the house and saying, "What do I have to live for now?" His hopes and dreams had been tied up in the older son. This younger brother could not verbalize his thought: "What about me—don't I count for anything?" Ralph had tears when he shared this story. Kristen has expressed that exact sentiment—*don't I count for anything?* Now, I too felt that way. What about me, Ralph, don't I count for anything?

We are all in so much pain ... Lord, you are the great physician.

From my journal:

*** *Carrying on.*

Did I mention that I'm tired of dating my husband? In my "head" conversations, I would tell people we are dating— many would be envious, Ha ha ha ... falls a little flat. (Dating without the passion or romance?)

What does LOVE mean?

What does COMMITMENT mean?

Do I love him enough to wait for him?

Or do I love him enough to not leave him where he's at?

God give me wisdom/discernment ... & could you help us out here a bit?

PLEASE—Would that really be so difficult for you????? ***

QUESTIONABLE THERAPY

Ralph and I both sought counselling; he opted for a psychiatrist, while I felt more comfortable with a Christian counsellor, Todd, a medical doctor who specialized in grief and marriage issues. As a couple, Ralph and I had very few people apart from each other with whom we could be open. At times we were a refreshing rain to the other and at times a dry hot wind. The issue of demands and expectations came up. Although I felt my wish list was short enough, Ralph felt he could not meet my expectations of him. From time to time my counsellor would try to speak to Ralph through me, as in, tell me what I should suggest to Ralph, which served only to frustrate me. I needed my own coping mechanisms. But overall it was a great relief to have someone I could confide in, who would ask good questions and empower me with a sense of hope and encouragement to continue on.

Todd believed in the sanctity of marriage; whereas, the advice given to Ralph seemed all over the map: "Well, if your wife is the anxiety trigger, we recommend in the usual anxiety disorder therapy, that you disassociate yourself from the trigger." We had some good laughs about the therapy we received. Ralph picked a few more advice givers, because he seldom went back for his second appointment, except for this one psychiatrist!!

From my journal, March 14, 2006:

*** I feel so full of despair I don't know what to do. Ralph and I have given each other a couple of letters, (one of the therapy suggestions to communicate without anger.) Also, on the advice of my counsellor, I had pushed him/urged him to live up to his marriage commitment and he said, "NO." He wants to be a good friend to me all my life—maybe we have a future, but maybe not—definitely not now. This is supposed to "free" me for greater works and more effective ministry.

Apparently, I'm not a bad person, but with the assistance of his psychiatrist he has been helped to discover that he has always been afraid of me. Where is that coming from?? Apparently, I'm too controlling, he hasn't been free to voice his opinion, because he knew what mine was, and he felt afraid to disagree. ("If you never knew you were afraid," could you have been? I really question that.) Some of the things said seemed quite ridiculous actually. "I've been in control of everything?" Yes—we each had our roles. I was in control of kids, holidays and home life—largely because he abdicated this responsibility, giving it to me. I'd asked him, encouraged him many times to take more leadership. DON'T THROW THAT IN MY FACE NOW!!

But I do want him to express himself, so now if I question him, he is saying he's not free to express himself.

NOTE: I bought myself a beautiful bouquet of salmon/apricot coloured roses & alstroemeria. I deserve them. Needless to say, I am a bit stressed out. ***

The letter Ralph gave me in response to my request for him to honor his marriage commitment, read like a final separation and divorce agreement.

Early on in our difficulties, one thing Ralph and I had agreed upon—actually, Ralph had initiated this—was that whatever happened, we should not change our view of us having had a great family and marriage. He had been adamant on that, and now with the help of this professional he was seeing things in a new light. This same man seemed to ignore Ralph's grief issues, *but* wanted him to go for sexual therapy. I wondered how many new *all time lows* I could reach. I put in a call to Todd, who spoke to me for an hour. Sometimes to vent helps a lot, but this was more urgent than my need to blow off steam. Our marriage was at stake here.

"We are living out our own life of dashed hopes. But with dashed hopes comes the possibility of new dreams. Dreams that are forged by fire, heartache and suffering are made of strong metal."

Now I Lay My Isaac Down, *by Carol Kent.*

Hope is hearing the melody of the future. Faith is to dance to it now.

From my journal:

*** *Wed March 22. I just read my latest entries—wow. Who is this person writing these heart wrenching episodes—how can she carry on?*
Oh, it's me?

Well I'd better write the next chapter of this gripping episode—
Will her husband return?
Will she move off to a distant land and find a new man
on a tropical island, where they end up doing missionary
work together?
Listen to the final episode of "As the World Turns."
As my Stomach Churns might be a better title.
Just need a little humour now and then to carry me through.

As my Low German friend put it yesterday "My life is a soap
opera." I told her mine was too. We had some good conversation.
Lord, walk with that woman. She spilled her heart out to me.
We laughed, talked, shared some tears and a prayer. God her
marriage has been difficult for 25 yrs—mine has been good.
She is living with a man she'd rather not be, and I'd like to
be living with mine. This world is so confusing. I had always
known there was pain, heartache and suffering, but I just
never experienced it. The difference is SO HUGE! I know it is
what separates Ralph and me from most of our friends and
now even what separates us. ***

Oh, Lord
How did you do it?
How did you survive the demands put on you?
People wanting the bread of life,
Desiring the wine of happiness,
You *did* turn the water to wine,
You *did* laugh with people,
What is this message of *the Kingdom of God?*
What does it mean to dwell within us?
Are you more than ten steps, or forty purpose driven days?
Can you move beyond the pop psychology?
What did you mean with have life and have it abundantly?
Can I enjoy my food?

Can I laugh, dance and drink?
"My yoke is easy and my burden is light?"
Why does it all feel so *Heavy?*
So burdened?
We all bleed red, Lord,
and my heart is bleeding for the unceasing pain of this world.
A father cannot remember happiness.
A mother weeps for her child.
A young boy's face is scarred by his father's hand,
Drugs and alcohol …
The sins of the parents visited on the second and third generations.....
Where does it all stop??
Too much pain, too much sorrow
Where is this strength for today and hope for tomorrow?

And Jesus said come to the water stand by my side,
I know you are thirsty, you won't be denied,
I felt every teardrop when in darkness you cried
And I strove to remind you, that for those tears I died. (Lines of a song from church youth.)

An enormous gap, a chasm separates our *knowing* about suffering, pain and disappointment, and *living* it daily. It had been much easier to deal with difficulty in an intellectual manner or vicariously through stories, which tugged at my heart. That was how I had understood pain and suffering up to this point. But, in the *living* it daily, where my heart had been rent, was where I experienced a God who personally entered into my situation. I felt His presence in the darkness, in the loneliness. He was alongside. He had entered humanity, to cross that gap.

CHAPTER FOURTEEN

THOSE WHO HAVE EARS TO HEAR LET THEM HEAR

Amazingly we can hear and see what we want to, what we are listening for, and miss what is actually being said. One of the first times Ralph and I went to a different church, we heard a message about "Not being a stumbling block." What the minister talked about was keeping our conscience clear before God. "Our conscience is a God-given tool to help us make right choices." Yes, we can override it, and we are not to be the conscience or Holy Spirit to others.

From my journal:

*** To quote the minister of that morning, "If you disobey, you will be sick. You will not sleep at night and your life will be a disaster!" OK, I was certainly hearing this more for Ralph than myself. (All of the above described him.) It seemed uncanny that he so accurately described Ralph's current state of life. (Oh, Joc, you are being self righteous here—and I despise that self righteous piety.) But, it did seem that the message was inspired. I wondered if it had the same impact on him. Just in case I was feeling that this did not apply to me, the minister went on to say ...

"God is the one who will effect change and healing in other's lives, we are not the Holy Spirit."

I was encouraged—and I was disappointed. As he concluded the minister said, "If anyone wants to talk more, meet me or someone else here in the front." Ralph leaned over, I hoped he was going to say, "I feel I should go talk to someone." Instead it was, "I have to pee so dang bad, I've got to go, will meet you in the back," and he bolted. Oh Lord, we are so human. I could hardly concentrate on anything after that, trying to deal with the disappointment. ***

We heard another sermon while visiting Kristen and Kevin in Alberta. All four of us attended their small church for Sunday morning service, and the topic was self-deception. The minister taught that *obedience to God's word in our lives was the true test.* Kristen and I began to squirm in our seats, both feeling uncomfortable with how directly things seemed to be aimed at Ralph.

"Why do you call me Lord, and not do what I say?" It wasn't as though Kristen and I felt let off the hook by the sermon. My own advice came back to me about not trying to hear the word for other people. But, as we conversed on the way back to their house afterwards, it was evident that the message did not have the same impact on Ralph.

Several times, Ralph and I heard words spoken that were powerful and relevant to his life and to our life, but, he seemed not to hear them. "We see what we are looking for." And yet he could quote, almost verbatim the story of the paraplegic who committed emotional suicide. The great danger and frustration for me was my ability to apply scripture and inspired messages to other people, and especially to Ralph. I was reminded over and over that I was not the Holy

Spirit. God is most loving and merciful. He moved gently, while I felt the urgent need for more push.

SPRING 2006 AND
THE BIG ANNOUNCEMENT!!

One thing I anticipated that spring, was a planned trip to visit Kristen and Kevin in their new home in Three Hills, Alberta. A fifteen-hour car ride provided plenty of time for Ralph's anxieties to set in, but at 10:15 pm we knocked on their door in relatively decent spirits. Kristen had been eagerly awaiting our arrival and prepared special snacks to ward off tiredness, and to set a positive tone for the visit. Kristen asked Kev, "Should we have snacks first, or give them their present?" To which Ralph said, "We get presents for coming here? This is a win-win situation." Kristen went to the living room, and we were instructed to keep our eyes closed. The crunching of paper was heard and then the "Okay, you can open your eyes."

Between the two of them hung a large banner reading:
HOW WOULD YOU LIKE TO BE CALLED GRANDPA AND GRANDMA?

Wow! "Yes we would!" Tears and hugs, and a prayer said for the new life.

What did this mean for us? A new chapter, a new sense of something we could look forward to. I knew Kristen counted on her parents making it, on being grandpa and grandma together. Both Ralph and I said we wanted to be grandparents and great ones at that. I wondered if we could get out of our own difficulties to be able to focus on this new stage of life. With God's help, I counted on that. It also gave us a chance to tell people some *good* news about our family. Far too long our names had been connected only with a sense of sadness.

Lord, give us joy, and thank you for something to look forward to.

Kristen and I had shared the practice of leaving notes for each other since childhood days, when I used to write lunch-box notes for my children at school. That practice continued and we would often leave a note to be found later by the recipient. Many of her notes after our own 9/11 (February 27), offered the reminder: "Remember God is not finished writing the book of your lives." Now He was also giving us a new chapter and it looked like He was introducing some new characters. I was excited for my daughter to experience the joy of children. Parenthood truly was a blessing, but I was also very aware of the great pain it could bring. I wondered if Jordan and Brittany would have a chance to meet their little niece or nephew before the big arrival on this planet? I liked to think so.

A nursing experience I had reinforced this idea. As the operating room nurse, I assisted in the Caesarean-section delivery, involving a young mom who had lost her own mother just weeks before the birth of this first grandchild. The baby came late and this mom had been told by her doctor, "if the baby is early your mom can meet her here, and if the baby is late your mom will meet her in heaven before she arrives." The grandmother had met her grandchild via ultrasound and along with this new mom, I liked to believe that the two had already met in heaven.

Monday April 3. We left Kristen and Kevin's in the morning and headed back to Winkler via Edmonton, where Ralph incorporated business into the trip. He connected with some associates while I participated in retail therapy. Recently my ears had been double pierced, I had decided to insert diamond stud earrings in commemoration of Jordan and Brittany, the April gemstone representing the shared month of their birth. Instead of a tattoo, which surprisingly I had considered, I opted to allow the brilliance, strength and value of diamonds to reflect my bond with my two children. (Perhaps in a few more years I will decide on a tattoo!) Anyway, I found the earrings while Ralph had his business meetings.

From my journal:

*** OK I need to write down.— we had a special moment this day. A big aha moment, definitely from God. We left K&K's house about 9:30 this am and headed to Edmonton. I asked Ralph if I should read the devotional from the Daily Bread. He said yes, so I was thinking I'd look for something relevant for us in the past couple of days. Well, I did not have to look any further than the correct date, Monday, April 3, 2006; the title was, Death cannot divide us ... the story of Lazarus being raised from the dead. (I had Brittany's small blue New Testament along.) She had underlined verses 25 & 26: Jesus said, I am the resurrection and the life, those who believe in me will live, even though they die, and those who live and believe in me will never die.

Such appropriate verses for this day. Not only that— Ralph & I are both crying as I read this. But Britt has written on the side of the page—Jesus is the Life — Live like it!!

I said to Ralph, "this is like a message from Britt," because if we had not been on the road, I would have been reading this in my own Bible, but her underlining of these verses, as if assurance from her that she was ok—not via a dream, but via the word of God—and her message on the side in her own handwriting, a real encouragement for us. Thank you God, the devotional was excellent as well. ***

I had photocopied the *Daily Bread* page into my journal. Some of the other words that were meaningful for us.....

Although writers and philosophers have done their best to marshal weighty arguments in favour of life after death, they have not succeeded in bringing comfort to aching anxious questioning hearts. Jesus, however, does not fail to satisfy us. He brings forth no philosophical arguments. He does not try to prove the reasonableness of immortality; He simply declares it! He speaks of what He knows, and answers with the authority of Heaven: I am the resurrection and the life, He who believes in me though he die, he shall live.

What does this mean for grieving Christians whose believing loved ones have died? Death does not sever our love for them, for love belongs to the spirit and not to the body. And when those we love go on a long journey, their thoughts can span the distance as though it were a step. Are you sorrowing over someone who has been called to heaven? Jesus promises that we shall be reunited one day, when God gives us back our precious loved ones. M.R. De Haan M.D.

From my journal:

*** (The next day.) Monday evening was less than stellar for me. It's our 6 month anniversary. It has been 6 months since he moved out. We stopped in Lloydminster for supper at a fairly nice place. When we got our water, I said to Ralph, "Let's toast." He looked puzzled. "Let's toast, it's our 6 month anniversary." He still looked puzzled. I told him it had been 6 months since he had moved out. In my questionable taste I joked with him as to whether he should get me flowers. He couldn't believe it in some ways. So could I let myself be quiet?? Oh No! When I ask (in my 'therapeutic voice') "Do you think it is going well? Where do we go from here?" ... he responds he is just, "taking it one day at a time, and getting some enjoyment out of each day."

I say "I do have a hard time not thinking you are being selfish. I can understand that for your grief your actions may not have been unreasonable (hard for me to say), but I don't think we can continue like this." The waitress brings our food—I'm in tears. She comes back briefly to check and I'm still in tears. "Don't you have goals, make a plan? Even in business?"

His response, "No, not really, other than for each day to try and make smart choices, and each day try to choose things that are long term good for business."

So trying to use that I said, "I am so afraid that you are making choices that have long term consequences, some days there is so much pain and the emotional damage and hurt is mounting; some day when you feel like coming back—I'll feel like saying forget it!"

He does not have the sense of coming back because "it is the right thing to do." He wants to want to come back. And some days he purposely stays aloof, to not give me false hope.

And I feel like I need all the hope I can get. Lord, keep me from self-righteousness—I know I have my own problems. The man I've been married to for almost 30 years, can still wonder if he should come back to his marriage. Today on the final drive home from Carman to the three-mile corner, I cried. Oldies were on the radio, the one that sent me over the top was a very melodious one...some of the words I think.

> I really loved you for a long time
> I've done everything I could to make you love me
> I'm gonna love you for a long time
> (something about you leaving)
> I'm gonna miss you for a long time
> because I tried everything to make you stay.

That's how I feel God—I've given him to you so many times—What do I do? ***

(In silence I faced the window, tears streaming down my face. Tears turned to weeping until my shaking body could not stop. Ralph looked at me and asked if I was okay.)

"*Let your hand be with me, and keep me from harm that I will be free from pain.*"

(NIV, 1 Chron. 4:10), the verse that mocked and encouraged me from the top of my journal.

I picked up Cinder from my sister's house. He was always delighted to see me when I'd been away. That dog was such a treasure for me, a real life-line.

Come sit with me Cinder
my husband's not home
Come sit with me Cinder
my children are gone
Come sit with me Cinder
I don't want to be alone.

CHAPTER FIFTEEN

REFLECTIONS FROM
JUNE OF 2006

Spring has long been my favourite time of the year ... bursting with more hope than flowers.

We were well into the second year of our grief journey and people expected that life should be back to normal for us.

Oh, how I wished that were so. A relative who'd lost an adult child two years before our accident told me this.

From my journal:

*** *"The first year was hard with sorrow, but the second year ... the aching, the longing and the missing our child was so great."*

It seems that aching can be palpable, like a taste, a craving that does not go away.

Friends asked us to go away with them, for a weekend to Dryberry. (a place that held a lot of special significance.) Our Cabin had been the most wonderful place on the planet ... but it was jam-packed with memories of our kids, our family, a much better time ... We knew the invite came as an offer of kindness and with nothing but good intentions. But neither Ralph nor I felt we would be able to do it. Upon speaking to Todd, my/our counsellor, he encouraged us/told us, "Do not feel pressured by what others expect or want for you. Many people drop out of life for two or three years following something like this." He also went on to tell me that during a recent Sunday in church, he had been overwhelmed with sadness for us. And the thought had come to him – he wondered if people had already forgotten how sad and difficult our life is – yes even those most close to us cannot comprehend the incredible loss we face every day. I told Todd "some people don't know what to do with us, so they avoid us. And sometimes I feel guilty in not communicating. Do I have to take the steps to stay in touch?"

"No," he said, "Those people don't know what to do with themselves."

Yes, people may think us rude, but we are still in survival mode. And then The Beatles song played ...

*Yesterday—all my troubles seemed so far away, now it looks as though they're here to stay ... oh I believe in yesterday. Why she (they) had to go I don't know she wouldn't say. I said something wrong now I long for yesterdaaayyyyy .... Yesterday, Love was such an easy game to play." ****

We ended up not going away and I continued to long for yesterday when all my troubles seemed so far away and so insignificant compared to today.

That same weekend a friend of our daughter's was baptized in church. The parents were also good friends of ours; we'd shared many family times together. As this young man shared his testimony, he included the impact of Brittany's life on his own walk of faith. Her genuine love of Jesus, her positive and caring way had often encouraged him in his own walk. Her death and that of her brother had caused him a great deal of struggle. It was a powerful testimony to be sure.

As much as the tears came, it had a sense of encouragement, to know that her brief life held eternal significance for the Kingdom of God.

From my journal:

*** *Ralph is getting a Small Business of the Year award tomorrow night. This will include a fancy dinner at the Fort Garry Hotel & he is supposed to say something. He has written a courageous speech sharing some of this last year. Lord bless him as he shares—may you give him the strength to say it. Grant the audience the divine moment and challenge. He is talking about the move from success to significance, and the challenge to strive to be significant in life and business. Thank you Lord, for Ralph. Lord you don't just want to work in us, you have promised to dwell in us. How Awesome is that.* ***

After Ralph told his story, many people came up to thank him for his courage and willingness to include something so personal; many men would not. It had been very inspiring, but in contrast with the high of that evening, we faced the drain of our personal emptiness in the reality of our situation. Ralph seemed to find a sense of peace and significance in work and doing good to others. (I often wished I could have been an *other*.) That evening I was very proud of Ralph for his speech, his willingness to be vulnerable in front of an audience of business men.

However, his anxieties continued, as well as his struggle to be a husband to me. Alongside every darkness, there was also an encouragement, or I would not have been able to survive.

Kristen had given me a little note, which I pasted into my journal.

***

At the end of the long road of distress and pressure and upheaval lies the possibility of joy after all. We may not see it at first, but God is at work behind the scenes. In time it will burst forth to warm our hearts and those of all who watch us.

The exit from our current state of difficulty is impossible to forecast; it may come suddenly or gradually. It may take five minutes or five years. Meanwhile, we are called to stay faithful to the One who loves us and will see us through no matter what.

To Fly Again by Gracia Burnham ***

June also brought about an abundance of perennial flowers. Another note pasted in my journal is a scrap-booking sticker that boldly proclaims:

***   *Just living is not enough.....*
            One must have sunshine,
        Freedom and a few
            FLOWERS.

Hans Christian Anderson

THANK YOU LORD, the flowers are blooming. ***

Why I Plant Flowers
Reduced to tears by the sound of
wailing sirens.
Emergency vehicles rush
Every one rushing towards pain
and hurt.
Something lost, nothing gained.
The trauma of life causing the soul to shrink.
And in response,
I plant more flowers.

If Brittany had been a flower, she would have been a deep rich purple Morning Glory.

CHAPTER SIXTEEN
SUMMER OF PLAGUES

The hope that dawned with the blooming of spring flowers began to wilt with the summer heat. Summer of 2006 arrived as a season of plagues of Biblical proportions, including floods, boils and simple depression. Scanning through my journal, it appeared that my most fervent prayer for the past twelve months had been a plea for my marriage and gratitude for Kristen and her support. Ralph had returned to stay at the house, sleeping downstairs. I wished for more, he felt this was enough of a challenge.

2006 was the year we *celebrated* our 30th wedding anniversary. All my beliefs of commitment in marriage had been sorely tried and tested. We had lunch together on the day. I surprised us both by voicing the thought that perhaps we should get a divorce. (Likely I wished he would assure me that there was still room for hope. He did not.) I didn't think we could go on this way.

Kristen pulled off a small celebration for us in the park of the neighbouring town. She had invited two couples to join us. Specialty foods were carefully and artistically prepared and presented, and it was good to spend time with other people who came alongside to encourage us in our marriage. Kristen presented to her dad and me, a painting she had done for the occasion in shades of blue. The scene is that of a wind-swept tree in the middle of a storm that has blown many leaves off the tree and amongst the branches is a nest, with two birds huddled together surviving the storm. That clearly was her wish and prayer for us.

We had as much celebration as could be mustered.

Bits from my journal summer of 2006:

*** Friday, July 14th

I'm having a good time camped in Gimli, sipping a cup of tea & listening to Ruthie Foster ... right now she's belting out a song about, "You'd better heal yourself." This is healing for me.

Now her song: I want to cry a little bit longer – pray a little bit deeper

Want to break out from the fever, I can't give up and I can't go back

I'm not giving up the fight.

Please Lord, strengthen me—I've never been as close to giving up the fight as I was on our anniversary .... Last night—a Beautiful Sunset— Thank you Lord for that.

Think I'll take Cinder for a bike ride. ***

The printed inspirational writing above that journal entry reads:

There is a big difference between thinking and obsessing....When we are obsessing, we are in great danger of being consumed by our thoughts and feelings. We might let our fear overtake us or let our past get the best of us.....Obsessing is not productive; it's destructive. It carves grooves in our minds that allow the tired scripts to keep running.

—Nicole Johnson

*** Met Mom in the Co-op parking lot, as I went to get milk. Funny because I pedalled an extra block to avoid passing her *house, here I met her in the parking lot. Mostly I avoided her because I knew she was going to my sister's house for Wed morning coffee, I didn't want to go. She asked about it. I said I don't think I will go. She looked at me asking, "Are you sad today?" "Yes I am." "Well maybe you need some cheering up." Yes, I do need some serious cheering up. Funny how I don't want to be with people when I'm sad or down, and maybe that is when I need it the most. ****

A creative note on pink paper from Kristen glued into my journal, it reads:

***　　Love you Ma & Pa

just came by to bring you some fresh salsa – I forgot to give it to you yesterday.

Love you both so much and have been praying for you both already today....

see you tomorrow! Love you more!

The entry alongside the note:

Thank-you God for Kristen. Hold her up, Lord—she is so burdened for us. Help us not to be such a burden to her. Restore our marriage oh God. Sure feels like why bother—seems like you don't care that much, why should I try? Help us out!

May your unfailing love rest upon us, oh Lord, even as we put our hope in you.
It's Sat. I'm struggling with motivation. Doesn't help that I have my period.
Lord, please stop my periods.
This week I've come across a lot of other tragedy........
A friend—informed she has breast cancer.
At work—we diagnosed two people with bowel cancer yesterday.
A co-worker's son died this last week.
Friends of family—the wife left her marriage.

Headlines in the paper—a 2 year old child wanders away and gets mauled to death by dogs.
A patient at work yesterday shared that her 29 year old son was diagnosed with a terminal cancer.
A little 9 year old boy in the OR said "My dad lives out of town & my mom lives in town."
　　　　Ok, this can get depressing.
Here's a funny comment Ralph had yesterday. I made a remark about us starting to smoke.
He said, "Yeah—We've already got drinking and cussing down!"
　　Yes, God—I recognize that I swear more—sometimes it's cuz my anger is so close to the edge & sometimes the OLD language just isn't enough to verbalize this depth of pain.
I dunno.....disappointing to see some of that in myself. But also recognize that some of it was just my old rules & standards of legalism from before......
I dunno ... Holy Spirit, help us out.
Do we keep asking you, God—and you seem to remain so distant? Or do we not see the little things you do? But God when we've had such a big blow—we also need bigger help.
I don't understand Ralph.
Sometimes I feel really angry at him—at the moment he seems a bit like you, God.
Yes, you tell me that you love me—but your actions appear to be the exact opposite.
Oh you love me, but do not want to spend time with me?
Ok—I've got to quit this line of thought. It is very depressing.
I'm in the DAMN D's of Grief
　　Despair, Depressed, Discouraged, Dead in spirit
　　　　Revive me/us oh God.
My plea in response to Psalm 118:25

PLEASE, LORD, PLEASE SAVE US. PLEASE, LORD, PLEASE GIVE US SUCCESS. ***

Gardening had been such a creative outlet in my life, allowing me to continue playing outside as my children grew up. It was a wonderful way to bring about more beauty. For me, there had always been a close connection between gardening and life. Brittany had inherited or picked up the love of horticulture and had successfully been employed at Foothills Greenhouse for the last two planting seasons of her life. Now it was a challenge to go back to that same place and see that the greenhouse gardens, as all of life, had carried on without her. Kristen and I visited it together. While Kristen was taking a pregnant bathroom break, Pam approached me. Even though Pam was closer to my age, she and Brittany had enjoyed working with each other. She let me know that the greenhouse wanted to donate perennials to the prayer garden project. My eyes teared up when I shared that with Kristen. Some renovations had occurred from the time when Britt had worked there.

From my journal:

*** *They moved the counter to the other side. I was glad for that, because I have this picture/remembrance of walking in and seeing Britt's beautiful smiling face behind the counter. The lady that served me yesterday appeared frumpy, grumpy, totally opposite to Britt.* ***

I recalled one of the funnier incidents of Britt's early days at the job. She was reading about plants, constantly asking about different gardening tips.

"Mom what is the stuff you put on your plants to get the hydrangea to turn blue?"

"Aluminum sulfate."

"Oh, I thought it was something else, I guess that lady's will stay pink," and then she laughed.

If people would ask about locations of where to plant things, she would be ready to give the answer they wanted to hear, even if slightly inaccurate. She was a quick learner, by her second season she actually knew what she was talking about. Struggling freebies, on their last root made their way to our back yard. Many survived with a bit of tender loving care. New plant varieties and locations were suggested. It was delightful to have her so enthusiastic about soil therapy. She was after all the one, who at age sixteen, persuaded a guy friend to help dig a new rock garden flower bed for me. She shared the delight of seeing the tiny tulip tips poke through the ground in early April. Daily we would search for evidence of the spring arrivals.

From my journal:

*** *The world is just a darker place without Jordan, Jamie & Brittany. Last night I dreamt of Jordan playing basketball. It was strange. And I was cheerleading. I was doing the "Z-Z-Z-O-D-D-D-DIA-Z-O-D-I-A-C-S, YEAH ZODIACS!" (Zodiacs was the school team name.) And I asked him "Do you say Zee or Zed?" Strange, I saw Jordan in his basketball uniform. Long and lanky.*

Oh, how I miss those kids. And today it's worse—being here in Winkler, I see Alex at the pool—Britt's age and I see the mom of Holly (another friend a year younger than Britt). Holly is married.

A thousand images, words, thoughts, keep buzzing in my head.

I don't want to do things. I dread going to work, but I know these things are good for me. Too much reflection time—also not good for me—equals depression. OK, I've got to go for a bike ride somewhere. ***

And then, came the disaster of the summer.

For the August long weekend, Ralph and I went away together in the little 1986 Mercedes Orbiter camper I had purchased. Ralph helped me select this Diesel unit, frugal, functional ... it enabled me to get away from Winkler, to enjoy nature for my soul therapy. Ralph wanted to ensure that everything worked fine, as I had never been very mechanically inclined. We returned after two days away, and because of the extra togetherness on the weekend, he felt he needed his space and chose to return to the apartment for Sunday night. He had technically moved back home, albeit, into the basement; both to appease me and to stop his parents questioning, "When is Ralph going to move home?" This inquiry was usually asked of me, not him. Ralph maintained his apartment, as his escape venue.

That Monday morning I woke about 6:30 am to the sound of rain dripping ... I turned over and went back to sleep; no sense getting up to go walking in the rain. About 8:30 am the phone rang and I got out of bed to answer. I put my foot down into a puddle. Picking up the phone I heard Kristen ask if I would be up for a walk. "Oh boy," I said, "I don't know what is going on, but I think I have a disaster happening here." By now I can hear that it is still raining, even though the sun is shining. I hung up the phone and went to investigate the sounds coming from the laundry room. The connecting hose to the washing machine had ruptured and water was still pouring out. I turned the tap off, but as I surveyed the flooded room, I realized it had been going on for at least two hours. I was afraid to look elsewhere. It was the Monday of the long weekend and we would need some help here.

Going downstairs, I discovered water had poured down into the basement, running along the space between the two floors, and then down the walls, mainly into the bathroom and the family area where the ping pong table rested. The fairly recent grey carpet squished as I stepped onto it, trying to survey the extent of the damage. I felt like I was walking into a news report disaster picture. It was a mess. The gyproc from the ceiling, overcome with the weight of the water, had started to sag and drop. Likely, it had been a lot longer than two hours.

Five hours later, we had managed to call someone in to vacuum the water from the rug. Ralph had spoken to an insurance agent who instructed us to take pictures of the damage, and clean up what we could. He assured us it would be sorted out. Kristen, Kevin and some other friends came to help. We tore gyproc off the ceiling, carried papers and valuables out and then transported the entire basement up to the garage. Fans were set up to dry the flood. The basement was in shambles, so similar to my current life.

From my journal:

*** *Plaster & mess all over. Almost want to laugh. But it's fixable. And I know it is not Ralph's fault. But I felt angry at him, because he'd slept in the apartment that night.* ***

It was as though I thought the flood might not have happened if he'd been in the house ... at least there would have been two of us, to hear the sounds; we might have noticed it sooner. What most frustrated me was, that he seemed relieved to have a legitimate reason to move back to the apartment now that his room in the basement had flooded, and this would take quite a while to repair. The entire basement needed major renovations. With the extra stress of the flood, Ralph certainly did not want to take more time to travel into Winnipeg for a counselling appointment, I went in on my own.

From my journal:

*** *Told Todd—I felt like I hardly cared anymore. I was tired of working on this on my own. The reason I had wanted Ralph to come was to have a mediator, Todd, as a neutral person to discuss our issues with. I felt we needed a plan for working on our marriage. Ralph just wanted to "see how it goes." Todd compared our situation to a harbor when the ships come in, if it is a calm day, you can just kind of flow in and nestle up to the dock, but in a storm you have to behave differently. When I spoke to Ralph, I said "It's like our mess in the basement, 'Let's just wait and see what happens, maybe it will clean itself up?' Obviously not—it's a disaster. We need to plan and work at it to clean it up." (I didn't like to use the word disaster—we have had a genuine disaster.)*

I don't know, Lord if I have the strength to do it. If Ralph were to come on board, then yes. I told Ralph "I'm tired of playing solitaire." He smiled and agreed on that one. He tells me he loves me, but love is not just words, it is action. This is discouraging just to write about this.

Feels like a nap should happen. ***

Some good came out of the flood. The project of the basement clean-up gave us something constructive to work at together. Men like to do things, not just talk. *Especially* not just talk.

The next plague – B*oils*

From my journal:

*** *So, Ralph was telling me he'd developed a rash on his left leg, mainly the hip area. I just felt he was being a bit "wussy" and complaining. But he went to urgent care to have it checked out. Turns out it's shingles. Asked him today if he felt like Job—now having 'boils' on top of everything. He had to go to the pharmacy to pick up some medications. I went with him.*

He asked if I had some shopping to do. I told him no, I just wanted to be with him. He smiled, almost surprised. ***

The inspirational writing at the top of my journal says:

> *Let nothing disturb me,*
> *Let nothing frighten me*
> *Let nothing take away my peace.*
> *May I wait with trust, with patience,*
> *knowing that you will provide for me.*
> *I lack for nothing in you, God*
> *You are my strong foundation,*
> *You are enough for me.*
> Teresa of Avila

"BE CAREFUL WHAT YOU PRAY FOR"

The last plague came in the form of an unusual answer to prayer?

Ralph felt that his commitment to our marriage would be different, if he did not have to fight the constant anxiety. He claimed that if his head were healed, his heart would follow. In many ways I knew he was trying, he hated feeling like a failure as a husband. And yet, because of the unrelieved anxieties, he made some choices that had negative effect on our marriage stability. So in my wisdom, I prayed for the proverbial two by four to hit Ralph over the head to clear his thinking.

Towards the end of August, he went in to Winnipeg for a tour of a different woodworking plant. They were shown a piece of equipment that he was considering purchasing for his business. He was with a group of about twenty business-men watching an automated machine that cuts and sorts wood pieces, using the latest technology to maximize the best use of lumber. At one point the person demonstrating, asked everyone to step back from the machine, as it was about to close. Ralph and another viewer at the far end did not hear the command above all the machinery noise and within seconds a large piece of intelligent equipment descended and whacked Ralph and the other man from behind. Not only did it knock them both to the ground, but it sliced the back of Ralph's head open to the tune of twenty-five stitches. All the blood gushing did nothing to support the marketing pitch.

I was duly impressed with the clean cut to his head and the good job of stitching the emergency doctors did. Fortunately, they used dissolving sutures, so he did not need to go back for removal of the stitches. The physical head healed, but the emotional anxious head did not benefit from being hit.

After some of the pain had subsided for Ralph, we were both able to laugh about it and thought that perhaps I should change the wording of my prayers!

CHAPTER SEVENTEEN

FALLING AGAIN

Late September 2006

Come to me, all you who are weary and burdened, and I will give you rest.

Take my yoke upon you and learn from me, for I am gentle and humble in heart, and you will find rest for your souls.

For my yoke is easy and my burden is light. Matthew 11:28-30 NIV.

At this point in my life, I did not feel as if anything was easy or light and I longed for the rest spoken of in these verses.

From my journal:

*** *Friday night — Big Mistake. We went with Al and Irene to a concert fundraiser for Parkinson's. It wasn't a regular concert — we sat around tables and had to interact with people. I left once and went out for fresh air, there is something to the business of smoking! (For clarification, I am not a smoker.) Anyways I came back just as Ken and Irene walked in with their daughter Diana; they came over to say hello to us. I hadn't seen their daughter for months. I was struck with how beautiful she was. So poised — she's matured so much in the last year and a half. And then I wondered, "Where would Brittany be at?" She was so beautiful as well, but lacked confidence and* seeing the growth in Diana, I longed to know how Brittany would have been. Oh God.

And they had a dance floor area—kids were up dancing and a few moms—it was still early in the evening. I was reminded of my birthday dance, watching how Jordan and Jamie had so much fun dancing. 'Where had Jordan learned moves like that?' Oh God.

Finally, as my head was near to exploding, I left again thinking I had to leave, I couldn't stay. By then three other couples had joined our table. I told Ralph maybe if I started walking home now, I'd be nearly there by the time they came by. (Seven miles away) And I left. He did follow me and caught up to me by the phone booth. I was contemplating phoning a taxi to get home. Ralph went back to tell our friends, he'd come back to give them a ride home. So I'm walking out in the rain in the parking lot, bawling my eyes out/intermittently trying to contain it. I'm reminding myself that I'm focusing on what I don't have, not on what I do have,

"OK, Lord, I've got Jesus & Cinder!" I said, and almost laughed out loud at its truth and its sadness. I know I still have children, Kristen (& Kevin) but they've got to make their own way, and they will. "They're having a baby and I feel like I am such a burden to them. Ok, that is not all true."

We're all so vulnerable and I feel I need to be strong for her. Oh God. Please help us. ***

Two days later from my journal:

*** Tomorrow we're heading off to see K&K. Bless our time. Thank you for it.

Oh dear God.... Yesterday Ralph & I were talking, he broke down and said

"IF only I could live that day over again. I would give Britt that ride to the airport. Why didn't I do it? Oh, how I LOVED that KID!"

"Oh, dear God. Release him from the burden of guilt. Help him to forgive himself. Wash over him with your love and acceptance. Give me wisdom to help him to forgive himself. Lord, he is not at fault. Please Lord, the greater tragedy here is for him to be shackled by this guilt. OH, Satan GO TO HELL. Leave Ralph alone! Holy Spirit, remove the blinders from the eyes of his heart."

My heart breaks for him.

He is not to blame, any more than I am—if we hadn't gone to Mexico it would not have happened either. We made the choice that day to let them go by themselves, it was most "efficient" as Ralph said, we didn't really know the roads were that bad, and even so there were hundreds of people on the roads that day, and the timing was precise in its deadliness.

"God, who are we to think that we have control over life and death?"

*I think this is the trigger that is stalling his grief. I am praying expectantly for a healing. ****

It was interesting to note how many people felt guilt over the deaths of our children. Brittany's boss in Canmore, wished he had given her more time off; Jamie's parents felt guilty, Ralph, me. We all felt that had we done something different, their deaths would not have happened.

But the ultimate giver of life and death is God.

"All the days ordained for me were written in your book before one of them came to be." Psalm 139:16 NIV

"Doubts are the ants in the pants of faith. They keep it awake and moving."

Frederick Buechner.

Well, my faith should have been moving mountains by that standard!

THE BOILER PRESSURE IS LOW

From my journal:

Somewhere in October 2006.

*** *Lord I hate the gossip. It doesn't bother me quite as much this time around. (This time as in that Ralph is again not living here.) It bothers me far more that Ralph is not here. Came home from Winnipeg, just wishing I'd be coming home to a husband.*

But at least I do have Jesus and Cinder!!

Had a good lunch with Debbie in Morris yesterday at Wilson's Grill. They do make excellent 'borscht.' I could see the pain in her eyes as I shared that I'd been thinking of going away for awhile—perhaps to Alberta, to see if this will help. Ralph is encouraging it, he wants to see if he'll miss me. God it's like we're playing games here—like high school relationships, trying to make each other jealous?

OK, it's late at night and I am not doing well. Decided to make some cards, to think about something else, I ache for beauty in my life. So I reach over to get some paper, bend over and then go to sit down, but totally miss the chair. I fall back and smash my head. I burst into tears, feeling so sorry for myself that Ralph is not here to put his arms around me. So I call him, just to have a mini minor melt down again. Told him no one is here to check if I wake up from a concussion—but I'd like to be dead. At least the cleaning lady will find me in the morning. God I'm a mess!

Restore something of me.

> "Show me ways to save my soul,
> I've got a hole in my pocket where it all slips
> away
> ...there's less and less inside of me, a little bit
> less each day,"

(Ruthie Foster song: *Hole in my Pocket*)

"*My kindness is all you need. My power is strongest when you are weak.*" 2 Cor 12:9 CEV

"*My grace is sufficient for you, for my power is made perfect in weakness.*" 2Cor 12:9 NIV

Well I'm feeling pretty weak, so your power should be huge.

*Good night ***

*** So next morning......*

Went to bed about 1:30am — Tossed and turned quite a lot.

At 5 am the phone rings. I stumble to find it in the kitchen. The recorded message plays to me "Elias Woodwork—the boiler is at low temperature." (This is an automated call from the business, when there is a perceived technical problem with the boiler.) My boiler is a bit higher by now.

At 6 am I hear the neighbour take off in his diesel truck, and then drift into a bit of a sleep.

At 6:30 the phone rings again. "Elias woodwork—the boiler is at low temperature."

At this point I realize it will be that and not a call from Kristen that she is in early labour, so the next ring I let the answering machine take.

At 7:30 after the same message, I call Ralph, asking him to take his ex-wife's number off the calling list. I told him with the first call at 5 am I tried to joke that "at least someone was checking on me to see if I'd woken from my concussion." ***

One of the challenging aspects of grief is its longevity and its ability to impact every facet of life. A return to day to day activities demands energy and attention, and provides a semblance of return to normal, even though the ability to function may not have returned to pre-grief norm. Ralph and his brother were partners in business, and a difference of opinion at work became part of the family Thanksgiving dinner, even though the brother was absent. I felt the family should allow Ralph and his brother to conduct their business apart from family opinion. The conversation escalated into a miscommunication fiasco, with a lot of words spoken on all sides, that left both Ralph and me reeling with hurt. Had February 2005 not happened, this type of discussion could have taken place without damage. The most cutting comment I heard was, "I know you've lost two children, but Ralph will just have to get over it."

A reading from Ruth Harms Calkin encouraged me....

RELEASE

YOU are showing me Lord
　　That when I cling to nega-
tive thoughts
　　Regarding the actions of my family
　　I thwart your divine purpose
　　And turn their actions upon myself.

> *I am beginning to grasp*
> *that I MUST RELEASE to you*
> *What I too often RESENT in others.*

And every now and then the Lord would give me an opportunity to show kindness, so I could pass on some of the blessings that had been extended to me.

From my journal:

*** *Thank you, Lord I had a good two days at work. I followed through on a nudging by you. Today was one of the nurses last day of work. She starts maternity leave soon, with an expected due date similar to Kristen's. After work I saw her in the superstore. I stopped to pick up some groceries; she was further down the aisle. As I went past the flowers on my way to pay, the thought came to me, "You should buy her some flowers." No, I was ready to leave and then I'd have to go 'traipsing' all over the store looking for her. So I dismissed the thought, rang my groceries through the self check. All of a sudden she passes me on the way for a pregnant bathroom break, she says Hi. OK now the thought came again. My argument, "Well she'll be out of the bathroom before I can do it" "DO IT NOW or you'll miss your second chance to bless her." So I rushed back, had seen some beautiful Kalanchoe cactus plants in full orange bloom. I quickly picked out the best one, zipped it through the checkout. She came out just as I was done, I gave her the plant telling her I had thoughts of my daughter in the same stage of pregnancy, in light of that I wanted her to have these flowers! Thank you God, for giving me this opportunity to bless someone else. You have encouraged us that we may encourage others.*

My other opportunity came that same day at work. I'd gone to the bathroom, and someone else came in to the change room. Through the cracks in my stall I could see it was Shirley. We were alone in the room. With sorrow in her eyes, she asks,

"How's it going?" I said, "It's pretty rough, isn't it?" (She lost a son this last summer, one who left a wife and two young kids.) There in the bathroom we exchanged hugs, shared our mother's hearts of sorrow for our children who had died. Lord you gave me a prayer to speak over her. It was a moment you wanted for both of us. Then I said, "Ok let's pat our cheeks—paint the smile on again and go." It is only when you have experienced that kind of pain that you recognize it in others and you can bless and encourage them as well. ***

For God Himself works in our souls, in the deepest depths, taking increasing control as we are progressively willing to be prepared for His Wonder. Thomas R. Kelly

CHAPTER EIGHTEEN

A NEW CHAPTER BEGINS – THE WONDER OF A GRANDCHILD

Kristen's due date had been set for the end of October. It was moved ahead a few times as she neared the date. Who can actually ever really know when a child will be born, at least when left up to nature? The brief time I worked as a nurse in obstetrics, one of the greatest challenges with a lady in labour was to call the doctor *just before* the baby was born, especially during the night. Please don't call them an hour ahead or five minutes too late. Of course, only with experience can you get a better sense of timing as to the arrival of these precious little beings. It did not surprise me that Kristen's due date fluctuated with each late pregnancy visit to the doctor's office.

From my journal:

*** *Tuesday October 24th 10 pm Kristen left a message on the answering machine. "Mom can you call, PLEASE, I really need to talk to you." Well, that gets a mother's adrenaline up. I called her back and she was out for a walk. Kevin updated me; "they will probably induce her—her fluid levels have gone* *down, and Kristen has lost weight this week." I could hear the concern in his voice.*

Ok, God, you are in control here. Preserve and nourish this baby. Help us trust you; the process is probably not going to be what we'd hoped for. ***

*** Wednesday October 25th, Just read a devotion on patience. As I walked this morning that seemed to be the direction from the Lord as well.
Jocelyn have patience with Ralph.
"OK Lord, like hasn't this been enough patience?"
NO, it has been at times. But mostly it has been a begrudging forced tolerance, not gentle patience, not the kind that says, "what can I do to help you?" Mostly the kind that thinks, "I've been patient long enough (everyone agrees with me) so you should be able to get your shit together."
"Does that count at all?"
Just as I'm having these spiritual thoughts of how lovely and patient I will now become, Cinder comes prancing up to me again, because he heard the dog-treat drawer open. (I was about to reward him for staying on the chair as commanded.) But NO, he blows it all and I want to call him a "little shithead." But I don't, because I've just had this spiritual warm fuzzy moment.
"Oh Lord, when the rubber hits the road, it is much more difficult. WHEN WILL I LEARN??"

Thou wilt keep him in perfect peace, whose mind is stayed on Thee. Isaiah 26:3 KJV ***

The anxieties for Kristen increased as her due date came closer. They lived in Three Hills, Alberta, a small town an hour away from the city of Calgary. Their hospital did not have C-section capabilities, and because you do not induce someone into labour without having surgical backup, her doctor was considering sending her to Calgary to deliver. As these concerns mounted, so did my unease. About a week before the baby was due, she was told that she had an oddly shaped uterus—a bicornuate uterus—she called to ask what that meant. (*It means, "You need a C-section,"* I thought but did not say.) It is a "heart-shaped" uterus and can cause complications in pregnancy: in conception—not the problem at this point, in difficulty to maintain full-term pregnancy—again not the issue here. I wondered if this wasn't unnecessary on God's part to add this, but tried to keep that to myself. Okay, maybe I did lament to some of the nurses I worked with. It added greater concern and tipped the scales in favour of a Calgary delivery. She was scheduled to attend a city hospital on Monday, November 6. Ralph and I had decided to drive part of the way to Alberta on Saturday already, so we would not have as far to drive on Sunday. And then low and behold, we got a call early Sunday morning, that Kristen and Kevin were in their local hospital. The baby was en route! What excitement! And we were happy that we were also en route.

From my journal, Nov 5, 2006:

*** *Well at 7:41 this morning, Kev called to say they are in the hospital. She started labour at about 2 am, and at 5 am they went to the hospital. When they called, she was about 5 cm dilated. I'd woken up in the night and prayed also—"Dear God, please help them have their baby normally." It was their hope & dream to have the baby in Three Hills. We just pray for a healthy baby.*

OK. I'll write it down here—"I think they are having a girl." (But of course they could be having a boy.) In fact, I even brought a gift—a pink set of sleepers. Ralph & I are both thinking girl. ***

The verse at the side of my journal from this day read:

"*Therefore the Lord waits to be gracious to you; therefore he will rise up to show mercy to you. For the Lord is a God of justice; blessed are all those who wait for him.*"
New RSV, Isaiah 30:18
From my journal:

*** (Still Nov. 5) Today I want to rejoice with you dear God— yesterday I had a very hard time getting packed. I had to go through Brittany's room to get my suitcase—I just sat in a heap on the floor outside her room and wailed. People want so much for this baby to "fix" things for us. In some ways, it is so much more painful, in it not being as joyous as it could be. It feels as though we are being robbed of the joy of this grandchild. BUT for today we choose JOY!! I told Jord and Brittany this morning they'd have to send this little one on her way already. We were waiting for it. Thank you that we left yesterday, and I could get over some of my sadness. Today I want to rejoice! ***

*** We got the call Sunday afternoon. K&K HAVE A BABY GIRL. We'd have to wait till we arrive to meet her and to get her name. Ralph said "probably some African name." I said "probably yes—but likely it has Britt or Brittany in there as well."

Keep us in your care Lord. ***

***   TODAY THE REASON TO REJOICE IS FOR NEW LIFE
*   MAISHA BRITTANY GRACE*
*   was born to Kristen & Kevin, Sunday, November 5 @ 9:08 am.*
*   THANK YOU GOD.*
*   MAISHA – Means LIFE in Swahili.*
*   BRITTANY – a life remembered, a beautiful character.*

Have you already met your namesake in
Heaven before you came down?
GRACE – Lord may she grow in Wisdom
and Grace.
What a beautiful name.
What a beautiful child.

Thank you, God. Kristen & Kevin are filled with the wonder
and awe of new life—so are we! ***

*** From Deuteronomy 30 (a collection pieced together from
verses 11-20, emphasis added)

For I the Lord command you today to love the Lord your God.
To walk in His ways and to keep His commands ... I have set
before you LIFE and DEATH, blessings and curses. Now choose
LIFE so that you and your children may live and that you may
love the Lord you God. Listen to His voice and HOLD FAST TO
HIM FOR THE LORD IS YOUR LIFE!

As Britt wrote in the sides of her New Testament in John, "Jesus
is the life ... live like it!!"

God I am pained with death, but you have given us new life.

Blessings and curses, we have experienced both, but even the
curses are broken by you.

Because You died—Jordan, Britt and Jamie have life eternal.

We were talking with K&K yesterday about the concept of eternity—is it no beginning and end, or just no end?

Were we with God before we came here to the earth? I'm not sure
about that, but I am sure that I want to be with God in Heaven.
Ralph is reading the book Things Unseen by Mark Buchanan,
the book Brittany was reading at the time of her death. In it

he talks about eternity in our hearts, the 'God shaped hole,' our longing and our desire. He asks, "Do we long for something, can we miss something that we didn't have? You long for and miss something you have experienced."

God, sometimes I just ache for you, I feel like the psalmist as he expresses, "as the deer pants for the water—so my soul longs for you." (Ps. 42.) I ache for beauty, I long for Ralph as well—because I do miss what I had. I miss being loved and cherished.

We are complicated creatures Lord, and quite unstable—Be my Sure Foundation.

Thank you, Lord.

It's about 7:20 am, I'm going for a walk in Three Hills. ***

From my journal Nov 10:

*** Words from a card for Kristen,

Having a Daughter
Means loving more than you ever thought you could love.
It means giving more than you thought you could give.
It also means receiving in unbelievable measure.
It means forever giving a piece of your heart to her.
It means no matter what you have or have not done in this world.
You have given the world
Something Beautiful. ***
(Author unknown)

WHO IS TALKING OUT OF MY HEAD?

HOPE AGAIN FOR PEACE

The birth of our granddaughter brought a new sense of life, hope and joy to our lives.

That Christmas was definitely better than the previous one—I'm not sure there could ever be a worse Christmas than that of 2005. Kristen and Kevin traveled the fifteen hours to Manitoba with six-week old Maisha to join the family for Christmas.

And Ralph was willing to try going on a Mexican holiday in January! That was something that gave me hope. I even bought something seductive to wear ... just in case.

CHAPTER NINETEEN
2007

From my journal:

*** HAPPY

    NEW   *What is happiness?*

    A   *What is NEW???*

    R   *How many more years Lord?*

Jeremiah 6:16 NIV

This is what the Lord says,
> *Stand at the crossroads and look;*
> *Ask for the ancient paths,*
> *Ask where the good way is, and walk in it,*
> *And you will find rest for your souls.*

My one desire (actually, I have many) is to be able to think beyond myself and my tragedy.

Perhaps I can bring some hope and encouragement to other people.

My main focus is to be able to have my marriage restored. Lord, how does one do that?

Perhaps my theme can be, "Think outside the box."
This takes on new meaning with both the above desires. ***

The holiday trip plans to Mexico in early January were thrown into uncertainty, as my eighty-three year old mother was rushed to the hospital thirty-six hours before we were to fly out. She had collapsed at the grocery store and was taken into the hospital by ambulance in a state of confusion, caused by her heart in atrial fibrillation. Should we go, or stay to see what would happen? After a night in intensive care, her heart converted to a normal rhythm.

My mother was adamant that we go.

The morning of our departure, in the midst of my packing, I went out to pick up a coffee and muffin and while driving I caught five minutes of a Christian talk show. The lady spoke about freedom from debt in marriage, but I caught her choice words. She had to recognize that "No, my husband was not perfect, but neither am I. We are in marriage for the long haul, and we need to have patience." The question she asked herself was, "In the light of eternity will it (my irritations) matter?" It felt that I had been given a message for further patience, and the continuance to focus on what does matter in the long haul, and what does have *eternal* significance.

We spent a week at a gorgeous all-inclusive resort in Puerto Vallarta. It was not all, not even nearly all I wished it would be; my specialty clothing stayed in the suitcase. But the get away provided something different, a new location, a chance to see a different part of the world and a chance to think outside our misery, although our misery and Ralph's anxieties had a way of being with us constantly.

One of the most memorable moments for me was my kayak encounter with the dolphins. While in Florida with Kristen and Kevin for the 2005 Christmas, we saw the dolphins swim on a number of occasions. Being prairie people, we were enthralled whenever we would spot their fins poking out of the waters and considered it a special blessing when we saw them on that Christmas Day.

In Mexico, at our resort, blue plastic ocean-going kayaks were available. The waves crashing onto the shore-line made me fearful of heading out on my own. To overcome that fear, I took one of these blue units and practised coming in to shore, to the point that one of the macho young lifeguards came to tell me that I was not to use the kayak as a surfboard. Ha ha, I thought—I was doing this as self-preservation—not a chance I was trying to surf!! Those young guys hadn't a clue sometimes. (And he probably thought the same of me; if the old broad wanted to surf, she should use one of the boogie boards.) Oh well, we got it sorted out in the end, and after I washed up on shore only once out of the last four attempted landings, I decided, if I wanted to walk on water I had to step out of the boat—translated in this situation, it meant if I wanted to kayak in the ocean, I had to get out of the bay! So I did. The second time out, I joined a group of ten other enthusiasts. Leaving at 10 am, we followed the leader as he guided us around the area. We were just returning to the resort beach area when someone exclaimed, "There! Look! DOLPHINS!!"

A French tourist and I turned our kayaks back toward the horizon and eagerly followed in the direction that people were pointing. After ten minutes of vigorous paddling we spotted them in the distance. Then we pulled this way and that way, trying to follow the direction the pod was traveling. Suddenly, all effort ceased and as if by divine appointment, we were among them. I stopped the kayak in reverence as two dolphins swam alongside me, then dipped beneath my kayak and came up about ten feet in front of me. We then continued in silence and wonder, following them as best we could. As a bonus blessing, we spotted whales in the distance, the spouts of water that sprayed out of black humps confirmed it. That morning on the ocean gave me a vivid sense that there are many opportunities to come apart, as we are often scripturally invited to do ... mostly, I'd been coming apart literally. Here was a soothing sense of serenity and eternity combined in the flesh. Pelicans glided gracefully just inches above the water. Waves kept pounding. Footsteps on the shore are washed away in moments. We leave very little mark on the sand, but apparently that mark which we do leave, has a way of echoing into eternity. To look at the horizon on the ocean, it seemed that the water and the sky blended as one; earth and heaven connected for me that day. And the dolphins ministered as God's angels. When we got back to shore, the French man spoke excitedly about making eye contact with the dolphins. We both agreed it had been an exceptional awe inspiring encounter.

"If you begin to live life looking for the God that is all around you, every moment becomes a prayer."

Frank Bianco

From my journal Jan 27, 07:

*** 23 months ago ... Oh Lord help me, help me.

FAITH— "the assurance of things hoped for, the belief of things not yet seen"

Today it feels like I don't know if I can make it. God I don't know if I can 'stay the course or run the race.' I can't even crawl.

PLEASE, please, can you ease up on us a bit.

OK, I am going to have to go and do something. It is not difficult to descend into the abyss of despair and self pity. ***

Part of my job as an operating room nurse involved being on-call for emergency surgery. As our hospital region grew in size, so did the frequency of callbacks. Earlier in my career, I could convince myself when being roused out of bed in the middle of the night, that I was thankful I still stood on the giving and not the receiving end of surgery. No matter the circumstances, I felt that the person in need of emergency surgery deserved positive help, which involved forced cheerfulness on many occasions.

From my journal, Feb 1, 2007, 4:27 am:

*** Just came home from a C-section. It's full moon. We did 2 sections last evening and now one in the night. It feels like February is starting off with a bang.

Help us. The wind is sounding at my door; fresh snow is falling. It's beautiful outside. In the last 10 hours I have helped 3 baby boys enter the world. The last mother was born in 1986, a year younger than Brittany. She (the patient) is 20 yrs old. Facing emotions in the middle of the night is not usually easy.

As I drove home from the hospital, I imagined you sitting beside me, Lord.

'But are you in the driver's seat?'

I want to know and trust you more, even if Ralph continues to live apart from me.

Oh, grant me wisdom, patience and Love. ***

Being a part of the team that helped babies enter this world had always been a highlight for me, although it frequently happened at odd hours. Now it brought such painful reminders of joys I would never get to know. Why are other people's children giving them grandkids and not mine? Many times in the operating room, we witnessed tears from a first-time dad, as he greeted this tiny little person, who was now his own. Who can see what happens in the future with our children? As I handed the slippery bundle over to the arms of an exuberant dad, I wondered how many of these teary-eyed parents, would face the horrific experience of the loss of one of their precious children.

From my journal, Feb 12, 2007:

*** Dear God,
Were you ever confused?
Jesus, did you ever wonder about the state of things?
Did you ever wonder if God loved you? Or did you always know? ***

ANNIVERSARYS KEEP COMING

From my journal:

*** February 18, 2007

Warring emotions rage inside me again. The heaviness of the Feb anniversary is upon me again.

I want to be obedient and love you
I want to lash out at Ralph
I want to be healed
I want my kids back
God WHAT SHOULD I DO?
WHAT DO YOU WANT FROM ME?
AND GIVE ME THE STRENGTH TO DO IT
I CANNOT DO THIS ON MY OWN

Reading Joshua 1:9 "Be strong and courageous. Do not be terrified; do not be discouraged, for the Lord your God will be with you wherever you go."

(LORD CAN I GO TO HEAVEN NOW?) ***

Well, two days later I had another hissy fit.
From my journal:

*** *The inspirational word at the top:*

Adversity is always unexpected and unwelcome. It is an intruder and a thief, and yet in the hands of God, adversity becomes the means through which His supernatural power is demonstrated.
Charles Stanley

OK, so I blew up at Ralph. He told me he was going away for a few days. Apparently, I had made the upcoming plans to go to Three Hills. I had arranged a counselling appointment for him. He suggested it was all about me; he just wants to wait till it gets better. Aaagh — I cried, yelled, threw things. Oh God, like a tantrum, I'm embarrassed to say. He remained calm — maddeningly so — but I guess if he would have responded in anger I would've said even more hurtful things. It's a bit like PMS ... you know it's coming, you don't want to do what you feel you might, and in the end it feels like you have so little control. I need a better release valve than this. (In my journal I have the apology note I had written to Ralph – HOPE written across it, and the words: Ralph I am so sorry for all the actions, words and pain caused with my melt down. I love you — Thanks for still trying! I wish for better days.)

Talked to Katie about some of this. Laughed and told her it's a good thing I'd been praying about it. That must have been really evident to Ralph!! Oh Lord, and then I felt like such a shit for behaving like I did. We are both so frustrated. Could you not help us out a bit God, or are you and I just can't see it?? Am I to believe that if you weren't helping us out, it would be even worse? I told you the other day, distraught and in tears— "Ok, you win—Do Whatever—I can't handle this anymore!" All these books, talk about releasing to you and then the Peace comes, I feel I've released over and over and over again. But the peace is elusive. Or is it there God?

I HAVE TO BELIEVE IN YOU GOD, I have nothing else.

ZIPPO—DIDDLY—ZERO—NOTHING !!!

Take my nothing Lord and make it something. AMEN ***

From my journal:

***

WOW

Life has been a crazy ride again.

Saturday February 24th approx 4:30 pm Ralph and Jocelyn Fehr, on their way to Three Hills to be with Kristen, Kevin and Maisha for the anniversary weekend, get hit by a semi-truck from behind. Once again, Lord we don't know what has hit us. For 2 years, I've felt like we've been hit by a semi, now we actually were. It's been 9 days now & I can't even begin to journal all of this last week or so.

But I choose to believe we are thankful to be alive. I thought Ralph had died.

Well, it's dejavu.

After the accident I did not know how to get a hold of K&K (from the hospital) as they were in Edmonton. I remembered our call display and that she had called us from the place they were staying Sat morning before we left. (We are in Regina hospital—Ralph is still unconscious.) Vicki & Ray went to our house in Winkler to get the number off our call display. I wanted to be the one to call Kristen, but tried and tried and couldn't get through. Finally, I left a message in a cheery voice on a stranger's answering machine.

"This is for Kristen and Kevin—Mom here, just going to let you know we probably won't get to your house tomorrow, we've had some car trouble. Can you call me on dad's cell phone tonight? Love ya, Mom." Kev thought the message was ok. Kristen said, "No, Kevin, that's my mom talking in her voice of 'I don't know who is getting this message and I'm not sure what to say'."

She was my biggest concern at this point. Can she handle a call like this? Should I wait till the morning? I wanted to talk to her in person. Debbie finally got through to Kristen and then we connected right after that. ***

*** Today is March 5, 2007. Two years ago, we had the funeral for Jordan and Brittany. God, I miss them. I've spent 2 years reflecting, thinking, questioning. I don't have the energy to do it with this situation. So I probably won't.

> The end of a matter is better than its beginning
> and patience is better than pride.
> Do not say, "Why were the old days better than
> these?"
> For it is not wise to ask such questions." From
> Ecclesiastes 7:8,10 NIV

Perhaps Lord, if Ralph & I can get on the battlefield together to fight our struggles as a married couple it will be worth it. May some good come of it all.

It feels as though Satan is working pretty hard against us. ***

I re-lived this event in my mind for weeks, like a video on replay. The accident happened with such speed, I only had a few seconds to realize, that we might die. In retrospect, it helped relieve me of the anxious weight I had carried for two years, that feeling I had whenever I thought of my children skidding on icy roads, wondering if they knew they were about to die, and what terrifying thoughts they must have had in those final moments. It was a relief to know it would have been sudden. And in *Grace Disguised* by Jerry Sittser, he conveys the idea that ministering angels were there to greet his beloved family members immediately. Finally, it was a burden I no longer had to carry.

We had been driving along in Ralph's finely built red BMW Excalibur. This was one of the few times he owned a new vehicle. The roads were clear with some snow-covered and drifting areas. We were driving near Regina in an area that always has ice and difficult conditions with wind and blowing snow. Up ahead I could see an area of almost blizzard-like conditions; it seemed odd. As we neared, we could see it was a snowplow, and the wind was lifting the snow as he cleared it, making it very difficult to see. Ralph followed him for a while, and then decided to pass the plow.

I remembered clearly how we could see nothing except swirling snow all around, and up ahead flashing yellow lights from the plow. Ralph must have realized the craziness of passing, so he eased up on the accelerator, as I was thinking this felt out of control. And then BOOM, we were pushed forward, and our vehicle started skidding around, always forward. Back to slow motion, in re-living this scenario it seemed that there was just white all around, and we continued round and round in circles like a mental anguish scene from a B-grade psycho thriller. We slid—or maybe were pushed—ahead off the road, and we ended right side up in the ditch, facing the opposite direction. I looked over at Ralph, he was slumped backwards in his seat. I could not tell if he was breathing. He did not move; he did not respond. I shook him. "Please Ralph, please, Ralph, PLEASE DON'T DIE."

I realized at that moment, I did not want anything more than for him to be alive and okay.

My nurse instinct kicked in and I tried to check for a pulse, listen and feel for breathing. I looked to the road— *Please, are we so far down in the ditch that no one can see us?* My first thought was to see if I could do CPR. Something in Ralph moved and I knew he was alive. I saw him take a breath. Then a knock on the window followed by, "Are you Okay?" I clambered out of the vehicle to speak to this man. I said I thought I was ok, but my husband was unconscious; we'd been hit, but I did not really know what had happened. I took in the scene; much further up the road was a yellow BISON semi truck. He must have been the one that hit us. He had seemed to come out of nowhere.

As the scene continued in slow motion, I saw that Ralph was breathing. I was told an ambulance had been called and already a smaller emergency vehicle with crew had arrived. They put blankets on us and we waited in the SUV. When the ambulance arrived, I was put in the back with a neck brace. My mind raced, thinking about Kristen, praying for Ralph to be okay.

A lovely nurse greeted me as we entered a small hospital nearest to the accident site. After some initial examination, I was told Ralph would need to be sent to Regina Hospital via ambulance as he was still not responding. They suspected head injuries that needed treatment not available here. As this lovely, about forty-year-old nurse checked me in, I spilled out my heart to her. "Do you want to hear a sad story?" I asked her. Not waiting for a reply, I continued. "Well do you know why we are travelling now? We are on our way to see our daughter to be with them for this weekend, because on the 27th of February it will be exactly 2 years to the day that my daughter's brother and sister were killed in a car accident on icy roads. And now I have to call her and let her know that we won't be there, because we have been in an accident, and her dad is in a coma."

Again, it felt like too much. I didn't remember anything the nurse said, I just knew she cared.

We survived. Kristen and Kevin came out to visit us in Regina, as did my sister in-law Debbie, bless her soul. It was so great to have her arrive. I think she came by bus, as soon as she could. She'd been there two years ago, and she came again; some people just do what needs to be done. We received much encouragement and support in the days following. Our brother-in-law Ray left early the morning of Ralph's discharge and drove the six hours to get to Regina. After collecting us and picking up a sub sandwich, he turned around and drove us right back. My nephew Joel who was attending *Youth Quake*, a weekend retreat at a nearby Bible School, stopped by to see us. Initially, both Ralph and I were sleeping, and Joel left a note for us. Later that day he came back, I could see him as he rounded the corner, and for a minute I did a double take—he looked so much like Jordan I was stunned. His caring manner also reminded me of Jordan. Thank you for that. On the 27th we had a small memorial service in a room in Regina Hospital with Kristen and Kevin, Maisha, Debbie, Ralph and I.

From my journal:

*** *From an email that Kristen received, prayers for us, from people Ralph and I did not even know.*

Sent Friday, March 2, 2007 2:45 pm

Hi Ma & Pa...these prayers were just emailed to us from people we don't even know ... you are being prayed for by many! Love you soooooooooooooo much, be encouraged. The story of your lives is not yet over ... gotta get Maisha. K

"Please reach down with your hand of mercy and place it on this family. I pray for complete healing from the injuries of their accident. I pray for the hearts of each person in this family. They must be feeling as though they are falling into a dark abyss and that is so very scary with all of their questions, doubts, fears and vulnerability. Dear Father, let each person have a compelling sense of landing in your presence. Though they see darkness all around, and are afraid that being wrapped in you will not be enough to sustain them, I pray for mercy. In every sense of who you are, I pray for mercy."

Another prayer:

"I'm in prayer for Kevin, Kristen and Kristen's dad & mom in this time of grief and uncertainty! Father have mercy upon this family who have suffered greatly.......heal Kristen's father and bring him out of this trauma glorifying Your name. You promise that you will never leave NOR FORSAKE your children. We are calling upon you to sustain them, and give them "the peace that passes ALL understanding." May you be victorious in this circumstance! AMEN! ***

We appreciated the support. It helped us get through, but we still felt as though we were living a modern-day Job's life, only we did not have his stamina.

CHAPTER TWENTY
DON'T STOP TO BREATHE

Life marched on, waiting for no one to pause and take a deep breath, giving no time to recuperate before the next challenge arose.

Kristen and Kevin came out in mid-March. Ralph and Kevin attended a Men's retreat.

From my journal:

*** *Monday, March 12. Just after lunch and I heard the phone. It is Dr. Burnett calling. She is the female gynaecologist I am to have a uterine ablation with. Eventually after years of asking the Lord to give me menopause, surely I have had enough stress to stop my heavy periods instantaneously; I realize something medically can be done about this. A simple procedure! Sometimes the Lord answers supernaturally, and sometimes He uses modern medicine. Sometimes we are just slow at learning. Anyway I am booked for this simple procedure. And now I am on the phone with her and she is telling me that "we've got to change plans." As part of my initial consultation back in January, they did an endometrial biopsy. "Well, it has come back with abnormal, precancerous cells, and we will need to do a hysterectomy." I am stunned, holding my granddaughter who is crying, and I am trying to ask intelligent questions* without being overly alarmed. Kevin comes up from the basement, takes Maisha, although I don't think he has a clue what my phone call is about. Dr. Burnett continues, "I know this may be overwhelming at the moment, but the ultimate treatment for you will need to be a hysterectomy. (I am thinking— Lady, I've just been hit by a semi-truck. I do not have a lot of capacity left to deal with other things like cancer cells, ok, pre-cancerous, but it still has the word cancer in it!) She gives me the option to have more time to think about it. I tell her not to cancel my hospital time for May 2, and that I will get back to her. I hang up the phone and call for an urgent appointment with my local GP. Fortunately, I know the receptionist and she can get me in quickly.

Long and short of it, I'm going for it. I know it will be a bit of a tough go, because Ralph will not be able to help much, maybe he can. Just when we're almost able to breathe again, it feels like another tidal wave, not quite as big. I'm thinking, "leave it be, let it turn into cancer within the 5 years it likely would, and I could be in Heaven in 5 years!" But by that time Ralph & I will be doing ok & almost glad to be alive again. "Whatever," God, it's in your hands, and have mercy on us. ***

From my journal, April 2, Pre-Easter week:

*** So much for my "Holy Mondays." I feel discouraged, defeated and I want to swear! It's gloomy outside, I got my period a week early and feel miserable. Yesterday was a tough Sunday. Ralph's anxieties were pretty strong, he had a lousy day. So of course that impacts me. The highlight of the day— Passion Services at the Bergthaler church with Tony Campolo speaking. He's quite a catch for this area. He was excellent, funny, encouraging. (I went on my own) Yet something in me struggles when people make altar call moves. Yes, I raised my hand for wanting to go deeper with my relationship with Christ. And somehow, I'm *left feeling manipulated. Then I want to fast today, to try to get more Holy and ready for Easter. As if my own efforts can accomplish something. In the end, I think I felt more discouraged than ever. Campolo spoke of "the power of Christ in us," as if I can rev myself into this power. Lord, I feel as if I've done all that I could, it feels so insurmountable. Then, when I want to just surrender and desire the peace of God to flood me, it still feels like nothing.*

So I wait for you.

Tossed and torn in so many directions, Lord—desiring to live a victorious life and feeling utterly discouraged. Lord, please comfort me and speak to me through your word.

Just now oh, Lord ... Verses from Gwen come to mind. I went to visit her this past week.

Pieces taken from 2 Chronicles 20 NIV ...

They *have built a sanctuary for your name saying if calamity comes upon us ... we will stand in your presence before this temple that bears your name, and cry out to you in our distress and you will hear us and save us ... Oh God, we have No power to face this vast army that is attacking us. We do not know what to do, but our eyes are upon you. Listen, King Jehosphat, this is what the Lord says to you: "Do not be afraid or discouraged, because of this vast army.* <u>For the battle is not yours, but God's.</u> You *will not have to fight this battle, take up your positions, stand firm and see the deliverance the Lord will give you. Go out and face them tomorrow, and the Lord will be with you.." (emphasis mine)*

Ok, signs of spring—tulips are up, they poked their tips through about March 24. Have had rain, even a thunderstorm in the night.

Jesus—as surely as the spring follows the winter—help me to believe that once again you will restore us.

PLEASE Lord, I want to live again. Just for today, help me to praise you in the storm. Thank you for the tulips and the robins. Right now they don't sense spring either, but instinctively, they know that warmer days will come. Thank you Jesus!! ***

May first and I was glad the month of April had passed. It used to be that I was glad to have had my second and third child in spring. The month of April was a good time to have babies; by the time kindergarten started, they were more ready than the children born at the end of the year. Supposedly spring babies also do better in school. Would the day ever come that Ralph and I could be less sad when their birthdays rolled around? I wondered. Life was full of so many questions. How does one commemorate birthdays, when death has marred the beauty of life?

From my journal:

*** It seems more so in the last month, I've wondered if Ralph & I will stay married. If his anxieties don't improve, we will not make it. A few weeks ago Ralph had a salesman come in and talk to him. He'd been in the Viet Nam war and suffered post traumatic stress syndrome, anxiety disorder as well. He and his wife stuck it out 6 years and then split up, and they are Christians as well. That was so discouraging for Ralph; it was for me too. Almost like—yeah, you struggle for a while and then it won't work out anyway. Why not just give up already and start a "new life" a bit earlier? ***

We are not human beings on a spiritual journey,
we are spiritual beings on a human journey
Stephen Covey

Frequently, I had my epiphany moments, where I grasped the concept of life being so much more than its physical appearance. But like many others, I would get caught up in the daily, and life became a series of doing, surviving, growing, laughing, loving, interspersed with moments of great spiritual awareness.

But, when tragedy struck ... everything was turned upside down. Everything took on new depth. I could not escape the question: *"Is that all there is?"*

I longed for much, much more. And I longed for assurance.

Eugene Peterson put it well in his forward to the book of Joel in The Message:

"When disaster strikes, understanding of God is at risk. Unexpected illness or death, national catastrophe, social disruption, personal loss, plague or epidemic, devastation by flood or drought turn men and women who haven't given God a thought in years into instant theologians..........

There is a sense in which catastrophe doesn't introduce anything new into our lives. It simply exposes the moral or spiritual reality that already exists but was hidden beneath an overlay of routine, self-preoccupation, and business as usual. Then suddenly, there it is before us: a moral universe in which our accumulated decisions—on what we say and do, on how we treat others, on whether or not we will obey God's commands—are set in the stark light of God's judgement."

CHAPTER TWENTY-ONE
CHANGING DIRECTION

(Skipping ahead to 2008)
There was not a lot of skipping done, definitely no skip or bounce in my steps.

I had always thought it would be difficult to live in a Bible-belt town as a divorced or separated woman. Since Ralph's move out of the home, I struggled to stay in Winkler and I struggled to leave, but I knew if the marriage did not last, I would move.

"I will not live in Winkler as a separated woman," I told him many times, and yet I stayed, while I thought there was hope for the marriage; and for Kristen's sake; she had already lost so much. Was the little bit of family she had left going to disintegrate? It appeared so, and I felt helpless to stop it. The rivers of despair came like a flood and carried away the hope I had tried to hold onto for all of us.

My journals read like a yo-yo, up and down; hope for the marriage, dashed down with despair, alongside many passionate pleas to God for supernatural intervention.

Even given the state of our marriage, I was stunned and devastated when Ralph asked for a divorce. He thought it would be better for both of us. Following advice from one of the many marriage counselling sources, I suggested we give it a year before we do something permanent. That year continued without much change. I realized I could live in a marriage if there was hope, but he felt it had died. *Without a vision the people perish.* At one point, after I had shared with a few select people Ralph's divorce request, a sister with insight and a psychology degree said she had never seen Ralph so down. Her question was, "Is Ralph despairing over the marriage, or is he just so depressed and puts that on the marriage?" I was not the one who could answer that question. There was no doubt that the anxiety and panic attacks in my presence were torturous for him.

I had a long-held aspiration to live and work in another country. This was not the way I had hoped that desire would be fulfilled. But....

Plans started to develop in my head about location and vocation possibilities.

I searched different organizations for volunteer projects, but true to North American style, they were mostly short-term, usually two weeks or a month and costing more than a regular vacation. It had become trendy in church groups to do a mission trip. (Exactly what we had done for my 50th birthday.) But I knew that short-term would not be enough. I recalled that each time I'd been away for a two week stint in Mexico, I had felt as though I could live there. It had been easy enough to get caught up in the daily needs of people and places out of my ordinary. I remembered thinking at those times, that I could have stayed had it not been for my kids back home. But now Kristen and Kevin were about to head overseas and with their departure on the horizon, the ties to stay in Canada had lessened significantly. That fuelled my courage to pursue this dream.

Apparently, there was a nursing shortage worldwide, and supposedly, my skills were in demand. Honestly, I wondered if I could pull this off, but it felt as though my soul was dying daily.

Only one thing was more frightening than going—and that was staying.

That decided it. Still, where to go, how to start?

I focused on places where I could speak the language and where my nursing registration was transferable, which narrowed it down to England and Australia. England had the pull of a niece; Australia had climate and distance going for it. In the desperation to change something, I started with plans to move Down Under, even its name had significance. It felt as though I had been down under for quite a while; perhaps it was time to move my body there along with my mind; perhaps physically moving down under would get my mind up and over.

The year was full of doubts, enquiries, moving ahead, stopping to question again and again, learning to write a resume (a CV or curriculum vitae as they called it down under). Initially I shared these plans and yearnings with very few people. Because Ralph and I had been the focus of enough gossip and speculation, I wanted to keep things quiet. Besides, who knew if it would pan out? But there was a definite sense of excitement that began to invade my disposition, providing the energy needed to work out the logistics and paperwork required for an exit strategy of this magnitude. A move to the nearest city, Winnipeg, was not going to cut it; I felt that I needed a real break.

From my journal, September 17, 2008:

*** *I am in my prayer corner, my candle from Rita glowing— the one with the cracked glass—the light from within reflects so beautifully from the cracked glass, symbolic of me she had said. So Lord shine your light in me. Not just in word but in* power. I want to know you Lord. Thank you for your Holy Spirit within me.

And Lord, should I stay or should I go?? Right now it seems to be heading more in the direction of GO, and it scares me, but there is some excitement as well. Right now, I've got an email from the Plexus recruiting agency that says a hospital in Perth would like to interview me. Aaagh. Was talking to Ralph yesterday, as he helped me download something, so I could open these attachments on the computer. I guess I was looking for one last chance for him to say; Joc don't go, let's give our marriage another chance. And it's not coming.

Rita had some good questions and comments— Bless her Lord. Think about 5 years down the road, do you think you will regret or rejoice with this decision?
Do you think this might be a gift from God—to have this time away?
And Joc, what would you like to do?
What would I like to do?
I would like to go back in time to pre-Feb 27, 2005. But I can't—so given what the past 3 1/2 yrs have been like—I believe this is what I would like to do. ***

From my journal, Sept. 22, 2008:

*** Sitting in the prayer corner ... the Lord has given me peace about pursuing the move to Australia.

But it is a mixed peace. One of the main anxieties is telling people what we're doing. It's still four months until I would go and I don't want this talked about all over the place. Many people won't understand, and I won't be explaining. So Lord, make this very clear if I should not do this.
I have long (always?) wanted to live somewhere else.
This is not the way I ever imagined it to be.

I think in 5 years time, I would regret more not going than going.

Oh Lord give me wisdom—help me find the right hospital, the right location, I have to trust you because it is all unknown to me, but You know it all. You will be with me as I go. And I ask you to help me trust You. And Lord, be with Ralph, I pray that this time apart will be used by you, for our marriage, for strength, and for his further healing. ***

Willingness, sometimes called risk, joins the finest journeys.

Maryanne Radmacher

Thanksgiving of 2008: With prayer and thanksgiving, I brought my requests to God and He provided some peace that came without understanding. I questioned how there could be peace, when mine was the story everyone was glad was not theirs.

From my journal, October 23, 2008:

*** Much to praise God for, God you are good.

I love the colours of the morning sky
With the slip of the moon – way up high
I love the feel of a frosty morn
And your joy within, when I'm weary and
worn.

Your word reminds me that you carry me when I'm tired. And Lord I am tired—so could you please carry me/us for awhile. Thank you for Hope—without it we die. ***

From my journal:

*** Later on October 23, 2008

Have been reading a book by Carol Kent, A New Kind of Normal. She had a chapter on vulnerability, choosing it. Encouraging us to let people know we are struggling and not to hide behind our guilt and shame. Well, that spoke to me. I feel ashamed that our marriage is as it is. I also feel somewhat helpless about it. I feel I have prayed and tried. I cannot make it happen on my own.

I spoke to a friend who lost a daughter. I sense a lot of anger and bitterness in her, understandably, but only you can help us fight that.

Even as I write this, I am arguing in my head about my own issues where I feel anger and bitterness wanting to creep in. No wonder you tell us to root these out.

Lord—even if Ralph divorces me—you will forgive him and love him unconditionally—I am struggling with that.

Do I wish a good life for him? (With me—YES—But, can I wish him well without that caveat?)

God—You are God and I am not.

You have unending Love and Mercy. I have a very limited supply.

Help me to seek after you, to become more and more like you. AMEN for now. ***

A job offer came after a telephone interview from a private hospital in Perth; both my excitement and fear mounted.

From my journal:

*** *Last evening, I received an email from Cathy at Plexus. She said they were pleased with my references and would send a job offer. WOW! I must say I felt more excited than scared at that point. Lord help me/us. At some point, I will have to make a firm commitment. So it's almost like, now I'm scared that Ralph will change his mind. Actually, talking to him last evening I realized he is still so very anxious, but some of his ideas are changing.*

I guess I'm thinking once I say YES, I don't want to regret it.

I've been thinking and dreaming for a while about all of this, hoping all along things would change between Ralph and me. Slowly realizing it is not up to me alone. I release him to God, but even in that I realize God will not force either of us to do anything.

Ralph asks, "Why are you so hidden God? Why do you make it so difficult to believe?"

I've asked those same questions.

I also fear that my going away will be the final nail in the coffin of my marriage.

In some ways, it is a big risk, and yet staying is also a big risk. I've tried that.

So God, is my patience too little?

How long is long-suffering?

Thank you God, and I now choose to follow in what I believe you've been leading me to. Thank you for support and confirmation, through Rita, Dorothy and even Katie as I shared last week, and Todd.

God, I choose to believe in my marriage. Mostly I choose to Believe and Trust in You! ***

CHAPTER TWENTY-TWO
A NEW BEGINNING.........2009

In the end what matters most is
How well did you love
How well did you live
How well did you learn to let go

author unknown

Kristen and Kevin were set to head to North Africa, January 22, 2009. I planned my departure for approximately two weeks later. The Christmas of 2008 had been filled with a strange mixture of anxieties, poignancy and hope. Last minute requests to complete Visa requirements had me zipping off to the city on a regular basis.

My sister Rita and I usually shared our theme of the year. We had both given up on New Year's resolutions. They seemed to be legalistic, unattainable and forgotten after a month, adding to discouragement. But at the start of a new year we often shared our spiritual hopes for the coming year.

From my journal:

*** Rita came by Jan 2 after work to share a cup of tea—it actually ended up being a glass of wine. She asked what I'd thought for the New Year. The song line that has kept coming up for me is:

"Let me not be ashamed, let not mine enemies triumph over me.... Oh my God, I trust in Thee" song from Psalm 143 **

And then the day of departure arrived ... February 3, 2009.

It was like a scene played out in the movie of my mind, from the book of "Who is Talking out of My Head." (The following was written as an assignment in a writing course I took in Australia.)

In her mind's eye the camera scans back to reveal a woman, early-fifties, sitting alone at the airport. It is as though there is no one else around. Does no one else need to get on a flight to leave? Is she the only one who is running away from it all? What does it really mean to be running away from it all? She is acutely aware that wherever she goes, she will take her pain and her past with her. Is this the best thing to do? She has known for a while, if this is how things turned out, she could not stay. Ruthie Foster's song plays in her head ... *"I've got to leave this place, and I've got to leave right now, da da da ..small town blues, got those low down dirty living in a small town blues, and I'm running out of things to do."* ... Two summers ago her theme song had been by the same lady, but then it was, *"I've got a hole in my pocket and my soul's slipping away."* Her best singing moments came in the wailing line ... she could be driving down the highway and when Ruthie wailed, she joined in as well, such force that came from deep within her, the wailing part of the song was never long enough. But here she was now, alone in the Vancouver airport, waiting for her international connection.

"So, why did you pick Australia?"

Why did she pick Australia? Good question. Her brother Curt laughed and said, she couldn't have picked a further away place to be sure. "In fact Joc, if you look at the globe this is exactly half way around the world; if you'd go any further you'd be on the way back." It was a long way to go wasn't it?

There were moments of questioning, but she knew she was making the best decision possible for herself at the time. In many ways, it was strange; most of her life she had lived for others or at least with others uppermost in mind, her husband, then the children. There were always so many people's needs to be looked after; it had always required an effort to make time for herself. There just had not been that much time for it.

But these last years, there had been too much time for herself. Not herself really, it was the absence of time needed for her children. The unspeakable void in her and her husbands's lives after the accident had remained vacant. Nothing could come close to filling it. Oh, they had tried all right. The first grief counsellor they saw had suggested they focus on other people's issues, get out and help people. That all seemed pretty shallow. Perhaps it was related to the amount of money they had paid for the advice. His first session was free, but they realized they did not need to go back there again. It was obvious he was not familiar with the depth of trauma that came with losing two children. Could she have done anything differently? If she had known what it could have been, she would have done it. She had tried all things under the sun, as much as she felt was humanly possible.

But, it takes two to tango and her husband had been unable to think clearly, let alone tango. So here she was. Just three and a half hours earlier, she had been in the Winnipeg airport departures. That had been the second most difficult moment in her life. She wanted him to say to her, "Please don't go, I need you, I want you to stay. Let us try again. I think we can make it." He had not. Instead, he gave her what felt like a forced patronizing hug, a small peck on the cheek and wished her well, promising to be in touch. How was she going to cope? He had been her support for thirty years, and now he was wishing her well in her new life. She was hoping this move would be temporary. Oh yes, he had asked her for a divorce almost a year ago. It had not happened, she had convinced him to procrastinate. Either way he had wanted to stay as good friends. She did not think it was possible to move from husband and lover to being *good friends*. How ridiculous was that? This move to another country had not been an easy decision to make. The three and a half years since the accident, while their marriage was unravelling before her eyes, had been like a slow-moving mudslide advancing with her at the bottom of the hill, feet cemented in place. She thought she had done all the right things: counselling, giving him space, and telling him she needed him. Friends and strangers had lifted multitudes of prayers for the both of them.

"It is what it is," she said aloud to herself—did she say it aloud, or did it seem her thoughts were so strong it must have come out from within her. Thankfully, she had luggage to find and haul to the international terminal. "These damn airport signs could be a little more clearly marked," she muttered under her breath, but what had been clearly marked for her in recent years? The last time she had been in the Vancouver airport it had been on a connecting flight to Portland, with her sister Rita, when they had taken their Mother to see Gloria. It was probably the last time Mom would get to visit her distant daughter there; from now on Gloria would have to make the trip home. That her mother's health was failing had become evident in the past months. She knew there were three sisters in the area who would look after things.

The overwhelming gratitude for her sisters provided an inner strength. She felt as though they were cheering her on. Her oldest sister had adamantly told her, "You have to do this for yourself. Maybe this year in Australia is just the time and space for healing. It is a gift for you—so take the time. We are going to miss you like crazy—but you have got to do it." A wry pause, then with understanding and caring she forcefully added, "*No guilt either*." Smiling to herself she followed the arrows for luggage retrieval, transferred her bags onto the international conveyer belt, and then confirmed with the attendant, "And they will be checked all the way through to Perth?" "Yes, they will be."

Satisfied, but still unsure, she realized there was nothing more she could do, and went to find the departure gate. She opened her new rose coloured purse, the organizer style with all the pockets, to confirm that she still had her passport and boarding pass. He had been with her the day she bought it along with the new pocket-sized camera in matching shades. The bright colour expressed her desire for new and cheery beginnings. At her last counselling session, she had brought two aluminium cans of Australian, Banrock Station wine. (Who drank wine from a can?) But she thought it would be fitting even in the middle of the day, to celebrate her departure with Todd. He had helped her through most of the past three years. "How long does grief last?" He asked that question in a rhetorical way, as if he wanted to assure her that she was still doing ok. "The textbook answer is approximately one year for someone close, but not as close as a child. Two years is the pat answer for huge losses." Then with a smirk he added, "And, if you go a day over that mark, it is labelled as prolonged grief." Labelled—she'd had enough of that for the time being. She hated the concept of falling into statistical data; that was so cold, so impersonal.

The seatbelt sign lit up, "cabin crew prepare for departure," and the power of the engines roared her into the sky and into a new life.

From my journal:

*** So here I am. On a plane to Sydney. The departure was surreal—leaving the house, last bits of packing, going to the cemetery one final time. I felt like I was watching my life from the outside looking in. I longed for Ralph to be just a bit of comfort to me. He stayed around, but only hugged me when I asked him to, and only said I love you when asked. ***

I fully expected to return to the house, and had hoped to resume my life after some time away. Yet I knew this was a huge step. My thought had been that perhaps Ralph would move back into the house, look after the dog, would be begging me to return ... or would it be out of sight out of mind? It was a gamble in some ways; or was it just facing reality? I had wanted to believe that our marriage would survive.

"Love is blind." The concept of how love, determination and commitment worked together to sustain a marriage was confusing to me at this point. But I do believe, that if all three virtues had not been at the core of our marriage, we would have fared even worse.

From my journal:

*** Not sure how long we've been in the air. Somewhere I lost my watch before I got on the plane in Vancouver. It slipped off twice and I should have put it in my purse. At least I would have a sense of time. Oh well, somewhere I'll get it back. ***

But what is a sense of time?

Marking off days? Marking off years? Always waiting for the next thing to happen? Wishing to be somewhere else? When the kids were small, it was always moving them forward to the next thing. Starting school, finishing the year, wanting to be in the next grade, them wishing to be old enough to go out on their own, old enough to wear make-up, wanting to be in high school, wanting to be out of it. Wanting a boyfriend, waiting to get married, have kids, and have them grow up. Life is always wishing for the next thing to happen, meanwhile, actual life happens in the wait times. And what is time? A quirky definition I heard, *"Time is the thing that keeps everything from happening at once,"* from a British actor on *The Goonies Show*. At this moment my life felt timeless; the passing of time was not marked off with known things to look forward to.

My arrival in Australia was wonderful. When I told people I had come without knowing anyone, they responded, "You must be very brave." Ha, ha, I laughed. Either brave or really stupid; in actuality I was acutely desperate.

Leaving that day was another event added to my growing list of most difficult things in my life to do. I chose to take the advice, that I had given Brittany when she moved to Banff, "do not waste time on being lonely and do get into the spirit of the adventure." *It hurts when your advice comes back to challenge you.*

God verified my arrival with several incidents that gave me a sense of peace and reassurance.

A WHOLE NEW WORLD, commencing February 5, 2009.

On the last leg of a long flight, while en route from Sydney to Perth, I watched the movie *Australia*—how fitting for me, I thought. The recruiting agency had provided an airport pick up, which was greatly appreciated. This lovely limo whisked me off to a hostel where I had booked to stay up to two weeks. On more than one occasion I had to pinch myself to verify that this was really me, living out this adventure. The accommodation was less than desirable, but provided a launching pad from which to set up. Largely the hostel guests were Asians with a minimal amount of spoken English and most of them were taking language classes, in an attempt to gain entry into the country. One of the other minority English speakers was a geologist who worked in the mining industry and we agreed that the hostel was "not quite like the ad." The *Closed for Repairs* sign guarded the swimming pool from fun-seekers, while pictures in the brochure had invited guests to join with others for fun around the pool. The geologist let me know that the pool had been closed for the last two months and this was summer! But the hostel had a great location, was within walking distance of the downtown area, and near a bus stop.

My very first morning in Australia, I used the *Daily Bread* devotion guide, amazed at the words I found for February 6, 2009. The page is glued into my journal. The devotional is entitled "Rise Up."

From my journal:

*** *It tells of the story of a Feb 6, 1958 airplane crash, carrying most of the members of the English football (soccer) team from Manchester United. The team was rebuilt by Matt Busby, a survivor of the accident. Today it is one of the best known teams in the world. These are the words that spoke to me:*

"Perhaps your world has crashed around you. It may be a deeply personal loss, a tragedy in your family, or some other great trial. Jesus' resurrection proved that He is greater than the greatest obstacles. He can rebuild your life—starting today. C.P. Hia

God can turn any difficulty into an opportunity.

Rise up—my challenge. ***

On my first day, I walked to the downtown area. Just across from McDonald's was an older brown brick church that seemed to be a youth hang-out. Two teenaged girls were holding a sign that said "Free HUGS."

From my journal:

*** *The free hugs brought tears to my eyes. My first official day in Australia I went walking downtown to the CBD, central business district. Met by a lovely young woman saying she was giving 'free hugs', I took one—she told me I was her first hug of the day. So much reminded me of Brittany, and her 'free hugs' in the video I had of her. The spiritual blessing—that girl had no idea of its significance in my welcome to Australia. I left with tears, thank you Lord. Moved on and sat by two female buskers—well one actually and her friend. She was singing and playing her guitar—I can see clearly now the rain has gone, I can see all obstacles in my way. Gone are the dark clouds that had me down, gonna be a bright, bright sun-shiny day. And then Knock, knock knocking on Heaven's Door. Lord I just feel you had your hand upon it.* ***

The verse I discovered, then personally claimed in Australia ....

God will create a new thing in this land:

A transformed woman will embrace the transforming God! (*The Message* Jeremiah 31:22)

In many ways, the move to Australia signified my desire to move on with life, and the acknowledgement that Ralph wished us to do this moving on separately. I felt very strongly that even though God had allowed these tragedies in my life, He was very much present in the current scenario and had been there all along. The struggles of my grief had forged my faith into a deeper relationship with God. But it had been, and continues to be a journey. Since being on my own much more of the time, I began to view Jesus as a close friend, the kind of person with whom I would have a cup of tea or share my French fries. Oh yes, I spoke out loud to Him. I did consider this a serious level above any former imaginary childhood friends. Frequently my sister heard me lament that, while Jesus and I had this conversation over a meal, "He still doesn't finish His French fries." It became a standing joke. I was so thankful that God and I could share laughter as well as the tears.

Trust became a choice I needed to make repeatedly. My conviction still bobbed up and down with the inevitable waves of despair, brought on with sudden remembrances of happier days and an overwhelming sense of loss. But I wanted to *live again*, not just survive, although survival is already quite an accomplishment. With God's help I determined that death and seperation were not to be the final markings on my soul. I wanted to dance, rest in the sunshine, drink in the beauty, listen to the ocean, and I needed to move away for my own healing.

She let go. She let go.
Without a thought or a word, she let go.
She let go of the fear. She let go of the judgments. She let go of the confluence of opinions swarming around her head. She let go of the committee of indecision within her. She let go of all the 'right' reasons. Wholly and completely, without hesitation or worry.
She just let go.
She let go of all of the memories that held her back. She let go of all of the anxiety that kept her from moving forward. She let go of the planning and all of the calculations about how to do it just right.
She didn't promise to let go. She didn't journal about it. She didn't write the projected date in her Day-Timer. She made no public announcement and put no ad in the paper. She didn't check the weather report or read her daily horoscope.
She just let go.

She didn't analyze whether she should let go. She didn't call her friends to discuss the matter. She didn't do a five-step Spiritual Mind Treatment. She didn't call the prayer line. She didn't utter one word.

She just let go.

No one was around when it happened. There was no applause or congratulations. No one thanked her or praised her. No one noticed a thing.

Like a leaf falling from a tree, she just let go.

It wasn't good and it wasn't bad. It was what it was, and it is just that.

In the space of letting go, she let it all be.

A small smile came over her face. A light breeze blew through her.

And the sun and the moon shone forevermore...

Ernest Holmes

(This is slightly abbreviated version of the poem, see further notes at the back of the book.)

CHAPTER TWENTY-THREE
THE WORLD ACCORDING
TO GRIEF

When does it end?

As I clip my nails I am reminded of Jordan's nice hands, the nails he worked at to help his guitar playing; Jamie told me that she loved his hands. As I shave my legs, I remember shaving them the morning of my wedding day, in anticipation of my honeymoon night. I also remember a sixteen year old Brittany cutting her right leg badly with a new shaver—a five-inch narrow strip of skinning that took weeks to heal. If I am ever tempted to drink milk straight out of the carton, I recall reprimanding Jordan at age 20, for doing that exact thing. In fact I now do it for remembrance of him, and for a reminder that some of the things I thought were important ... aren't.

When does it end?

I recalled many insignificant daily occurrences that stirred up painful memories. Why did my remembrances always go to those things that no longer were or no longer could be? I didn't usually think of Kristen as a child with these issues.

I concluded that it was because Kristen was still alive; she was making new memories, so it was permissible to forget some of the old ones. But for my children that are no longer on the planet, the memories needed to stay alive, because there would never, be new ones here in this lifetime, not ever. The finality is so difficult in the grieving process. All the daily little things can be painful reminders. The ability to put these recollections into the beautiful classification in my mind takes practice. In time, I expect to see the greater beauty of the memories, without the enormous sense of loss. Early on Ralph assured me that our memories were just as valid and relevant as those with offspring that were still alive. But as a griever, I soon realized that it was less awkward for me and for my friends if I did not speak as often of Jordan and Brittany.

Difficult answers to simple questions ...

In the aftermath of grief, when I began to pick up the pieces and move on, I still got stumped with simple questions, especially when meeting new people.

The one many of us parents, who have lost children, struggle with is the simple query:

A. "Do you have children?"

That of course leads to the next question:

B. "How many?"

And then if you've gotten this far it's:

C. "So what are they up to now?"

The first question is a simple "Yes" or "No" to the person asking the question. They are surprised when I hesitate to answer. And I am scrambling in my head, "How will I answer question B?" Do I mention my deceased children or not? Do these people want the truth? Do I want to open myself up to them? When I answer "yes" to question A, and think I don't want this to go anywhere else, I say "I have a daughter in

Africa, and three lovely little grandchildren." That brings the focus on a positive thing—like my sweet grand kids.

Once when I was at question B with a lady I had recently met in Australia, as I hesitated to answer, Madeleine looked at me and joked, "What, you don't know how many children you have? Is it that many you've lost count?" She turned deathly silent when I said, "I guess I had three, but only one is alive." People are stopped in their tracks, and then sometimes they awkwardly try to comfort or ask more questions. If it's another mother, she is usually quite choked up and teary.

I could say, "My two youngest live so far away that I have lost touch with them."

But that is not what I want to say. A few issues arise out of this scenario.

I do not want other people to feel uncomfortable, as they invariably do if I mention my two youngest children, but I want to honour my children; to not mention them seems not to acknowledge them.

I am also aware that I want to protect myself. I do not always know if I can handle the telling of my story.

It has grown better with time.

Who would ever think that this most simple and ordinary query could be so complicated?

Can anyone hear me?

I woke up to this haunting question from a song on the radio: "Can anyone hear me?"

The relentless uncertainty of the ages. Do I matter at all? Is my life making a difference?

From my Journal: March 21, 2009

*** *Lord here I am again.*

Here is something I am struggling with — I am not important to anyone (I know that's not true) But, given my most important relationships on earth: My husband, I feel rejection, two of my three children I've lost, Kristen is married and independent. Even Cinder, who has been my comfort for 3 years, I left him in Ralph's care, and he has passed him on to a family. I know it will be good for Cinder. I miss being #1 to someone or something, even if it's a dog. My self esteem is not high in many areas. And then my new job; I've taken away the familiarity of my work at BTHC. And here I am a nobody. And that's ok, I wanted to be anonymous. And yet as I say that I realize how painful it is. Oh Lord, and I just read in Isaiah 51:

"For I am God, your very own God." how personal, but what am I to you?

You've literally got millions of people to look after. And yet--Thank-You--YOU truly have been my sustenance and my strength.

PS Could you say hello to Britt, Jordan and Jamie. Oh I missed them this week. ***

I wonder at the purpose of telling my story. Yet, I had a sense from the early days of walking the park path, that someday I would need to tell my story. I know I searched for books written by people who had experienced a similar loss.

"Many people have suffered, and many have had even greater tragedies than mine."

In most conversations I hesitate to bring up my scenario as I have found that people can be overcome with the immensity of my tragedy, accompanied with a guilty relief that their story was not as traumatic.

And yet, whatever you are suffering at the time, it seems so great. When you are in pain, it does not matter that someone else is in greater or less pain. This is not a comparison game. When it comes to tragedies, there can be a sense of outdoing others in telling tragic stories, especially if it is something we have *heard*. If we have *lived* it, there is absolutely no desire to be the one with the most horrific story.

I wish this was not my story.

But it is, and I share it with the hope and prayer that someone else will be encouraged.

We all have stories to tell, and it is what Christ did best.

When we are crying out, "Can anybody hear me; does anyone care,"

I think we are actually crying out to God—"Can you hear me and do you care?"

I'll look today on the pain of my life as an artistic gift— perhaps a gift not intended for me, but for others. I will write on the hunch that this might be so.

Susan Shaughnessy

Walking on Alligators

Can anyone identify me?

When I go to an event where name tags are required, I say I need to wear a badge in order to remember who I am. The jest is closer to the truth than people know. Most of us understand who we are, by the roles we play and the relationships connected to those roles.

Until 2005 I had been: a wife, a mother, a friendly person in the community, an efficient operating room nurse, the boss's wife, a victim support worker, a Sunday school teacher, and the lady asked to give the church wedding shower devotional. After the accident, I felt an incredible loss of my identity. Initially I did not understand what had happened to me in that regard. Many times, I felt like a character in a scenario in my head. The grief years have been surreal, almost the sense of a *Matrix* existence.

Was I functioning, or just roleplaying?

My lines had been rehearsed, but it was not so much of a rehearsal, as a responding in a manner in which I thought my character should respond. I relied on theoretical methods of coping, to allow the emergence of my self and my faith to be forged stronger in the face of loss. This was not just the proverbial when the rubber hits the road; in essence, for me this was a matter of life and death, a matter of survival.

There remains a lingering sense of living my life as a performer in a play, in a role that I did not want. Most of the characters that I would have chosen to play, have already been written out of the script. Who wants to land the part of the real life grieving mother? Not me ... the *Get married, have kids and live happily ever after*, that I thought was going to be my life, was gone.

Although I felt too old to be trying to *find myself*, I needed to do just that. I needed to know who I was and what purpose my life had. The roles connected with family and faith, had always given me my deepest sense of calling and purpose. Now even my role as a child of God was in question. Would I ever inflict this amount of pain on my children, or on anyone I claimed to love? With my belief that actions speak louder than words, I struggled to believe the *loving* of God. God revitalized me and responded to my identity crisis with words from The Message:

It's in Christ that we find out who we are and what we are living for. Ephesians 1:11

Where you are right now is God's place for you. Live and obey and love and believe right there. God, not your marital status, defines your life. 1Corinthians 7:17

My life needed redefining and reshaping. I chose to begin forging a new me in Australia.

And I also chose to believe that when one thing was taken away, there was still another option, and when two or three or multiple things have been taken away, there is the opportunity to *live in the wastefulness of grace.* (from Paul Young—*The Shack, back cover*)

Catastrophic loss is like undergoing an amputation of our identity. It is not like the literal amputation of a limb. Rather it is more like the amputation of the self from the self. But it is not simply the loss of identity that causes the problem. It is also the difficult conditions under which a new identity must be formed. One cannot escape it simply by finding a new spouse, a new job, a new life.

Jerry Sittser *A Grace Disguised*

Time travellers

Isn't it marvellous in the movies when a subtitle says, 5 *years later?* We are instantaneously transported five years ahead, without having to go through the pain of the journey.

About the tenth day in our tragedy, I told my mother I wanted to be a year down the road, thinking I'd be in a better spot. At the first anniversary, she reminded me of my words, to which I then more knowingly replied, "I think I need to be at the five-year mark." Grief has a cumulative effect. At times other sojourners in this grief walk assured me that "it's still early in the process," this worked both to assure me and to discourage me. There is no accurate time-line for the eternity of grief.

On his hundredth birthday celebration, a well seasoned man from my hometown said, "*Some decades are hard.*" Unfortunately, I now understood.

I never desired to have this much comprehension of first-hand grief. I wanted to be able to experience some things vicariously ... through books or movies. We are drawn to story lines where the characters overcome extraordinary adversity, especially those based on true life events. Arm chair tragedy is how many of us prefer to experience depth of feeling.

Remembering birthdays
April 2010
Today would be my son's 27th birthday if he were still on this planet. It is hard to know what to do with these significant days. I started by getting out of bed, thinking to celebrate the privilege that I had almost 22 years to be a mother to a son as fine as Jordan. He was a most remarkable, but ordinary young man who had been a wonderful son, easy to love, fun-loving, kind and caring, he still hugged his mother. I often told people, that he was the kind of man I would like my daughters to marry. But he will never marry or have children. A month after the accident, a well meaning friend told me that according to scripture, some of the good people are taken early to avoid all the pain and hassle of life.

The righteous are taken away to be spared from evil. Those who walk uprightly enter into peace; they find rest as they lie in death. Isaiah 57:1,2 NIV

I did not find that verse as comforting as it was intended. If we want to avoid all the pain of life, why bother living, why bother to give birth?

So, it is Jordan's birthday. He would be 27 and his sister would soon be 25. I wonder what heaven is like, do they celebrate birthdays? Or do they celebrate your death day as the first day of the rest of your life, which is now eternal?

There is a magnet on my fridge that says, "May *you LIVE everyday of your life.*" Many of us just exist; I am as guilty of it as anyone else. When these days of significance come around I am extra sensitive and aware of the jealousy I have of people whose children are still alive and well. When people send me invitations to their children's weddings, it reminds me again that I will not have that privilege. We all experience some pain in life, but it is easy to think that some people have a lighter load. On my son's birthday, I want to remember that a number of years ago I told God I would *"choose Life."*

Today I am thankful for Jordan David Isaac.

I am thankful for the goodness I saw in his life.

I am thankful for the promise from God that we will see each other again.

It is a nice day out here in Australia, and I think I might go for a walk.

> *THE PAIN PASSES THROUGH*
> *I have to let the pain have its way.*
> *The pain has to pass through me*
> *So we can both move on.*
> *Every year has special days that I cannot ignore.*
> *I have decided not to fight*
> *but to let it pass through.*
> *Let the tears flow ...*
> *Let the sadness show,*
> *Then pick up my pallet*
> *And move on.*
> *I still have much to move on to,*
> *More mountains to climb,*
> *More beauty to find,*
> *Grand babies to delight in*
> *Holy spots to dance in*
> *New memories to make.*
> *Old ones to ponder*
> *And spirits to wander.*

Even time to squander.
Time to stoop and drink
Deeply from the beauty around
Taking in the sights, the smells, the sound
The sound of silence when I'm all alone.
Your presence with me wherever I roam.
With you, the mountain can be climbed.
The spirit refreshed and refined.
And the pain moves on......
And so do I.

WAS THIS IN THE SCRIPT?

This is not how I thought it would be, not what I had planned or hoped for. What about all the people who had prayed for us, for our marriage, what happened to all those prayers, God?

I know I am not the first; generations have struggled with unanswered prayer.

We ask for something in Jesus name—we are encouraged to pray, we feel the spirit leading us to pray for certain things ... then it seems to go all wrong, and we try to explain it away with "Perhaps it was not God's will?"

Then, we are encouraged to "go back and examine ourselves again. Perhaps we were praying selfishly."

For, "God always answers prayers, but it may not be in the way we expect."

I frequently felt the need to cover up for God.

"Prayer changes people, not things," ... That is the palatable response for the devout believer who has been following the way, but still is in an extremely difficult situation.

It is even better when we use scripture to mask our confusion.

"My thoughts are not your thoughts, neither are your ways my ways," declares the Lord.

Isaiah 55:8 NIV

"Do you who live in eternity, hear the prayers of those of us who live in time?"

Rich Mullins, song, *Playing Hard to get*

HOLDING ON TO PRAYER

What am I holding on to and why can't I let go?
Holding on to evaporated dreams gone missing,
Holding on to promises of love, deserted in the storm.
I am holding on to the quest for beauty, in the midst of ugly.
I am holding on to hope, in the midst of hopelessness.
I am holding on to you God.
But wondering if your love will fail, if you will bail?
Will your promises fall flat?
In my head I know ... in my heart I doubt.
A thousand petitions that I have given voice to,
In my groanings I have followed the rules of prayer
Tripping over the caveats added for disaster.
Pray specifically, pray in God's will, pray scripture,
Pray without ceasing, pray about everything,
Do not be anxious, but pray ...
    pray ... Pray ... PRAY
Prayer changes people not things.
Does prayer not change a thing?
When so much is at stake?
Can you know the desperation of my heart and still be deaf?
I am given the same answer given to Job.
And ... I am silent.
YOU are God and I am not.
You hold the trump card.

But you do not crush me with it ...
You allow me to turn it over.
And it always is the King of Hearts.

CHAPTER TWENTY-FOUR
CAN THERE BE A CONCLUSION?

Frequently I am asked, "So, how are you doing now?"

And I say that there are many things in my life that I would not have chosen, but I still choose to seek out beauty. The road through Grief seems unending. I am not sure if you can get through to the other side of grief. I believe this deep sorrow will linger with me for the rest of my earthly days. The pain, however, does lessen.

There are many choices I can make along the way to help cope with the heartache.

Much of it has been a Solitary Journey, although, many have come alongside to lighten my load and to help me walk when I felt I could not go on myself. You do, however, have to deal with the voices inside your head. You can try drowning them out, but the clamour gets too much, and eventually you have to work through the issues they raise.

After a serious bout with malaria in Africa, Kristen stated, "I do not want to go through this much pain without having learned all that God wants for me, and to become a better person for it." Given the choice, I would not have signed up for this amount of pain. I have been changed in the process.

And the choices made in small matters, in small situations in grief, are what lead up to the final result, if you can call it a result. Even at my age I have the challenge to make daily choices to be the person I want to be and to live a joyous life. And I am humbled that the creator of the universe has walked alongside.

And when the pot of tear soup comes out again, I take a little time to reflect on it, on how life would be and still wonder and will continue to wonder ... "Where would Brittany or Jordan or Jamie be at this stage of life?" But I cannot stay in this mind set for too long, so I put the lid on the soup pot and move outdoors in my mind, to see beauty, choosing to be thankful for the brief time I had with them.

I choose to hear the birds sing.

I choose to enjoy the flowers.

I choose to put a smile on my face.

I choose to believe that I can bloom again.

I choose to encourage someone else along the way.

And I choose to believe that God is good.

I CHOOSE LIFE.

WHAT IS GRIEF ??
It is not a sentiment,
of heart wrenching beautiful words.
It is incredible pain,
A darkness I cannot breathe in.
A tangible taste I cannot brush away.
A pain I think I cannot survive
It is not pretty
But it can bring about beauty.
It is a journey
I did not choose to embark on.
Grief is questions and searching
It redefines my soul.
Grief is so lonely
I doubt the existence of love.
Divine love acknowledges my longing.
Bizarrely, the sun still shines in the
midst of grief,
And flowers still bloom.
Because of that
I choose to live!

October 2010

As I have re-read my journals, I have been encouraged to see the strength of the Lord in all circumstances.

In the darkest moments, when it seemed all of Heaven was silent, I have not been alone. God has been with me in my loneliness, and the melody of the Spirit has comforted my soul.

And I still wish Jesus would eat His share of the French fries.

To quote my still-on-the-planet daughter Kristen:

The story of my life is not over yet, the final chapters have not been written.

NOTES

Author's Note:

This is a self published book. While effort has been made to credit all sources used, and permission has been sought, not all quoted persons/publishers responded to my request for permission to use their words in this book.

If your words or songs have been quoted, I want to say how grateful I am for the encouragement they brought to me during a very difficult time in my life.

Follow the author's blog site @

http://whoistalking.wordpress.com

Feel free to leave a comment.

REFERENCES

Alcorn, Randy. *Heaven*. Carol Stream, Illinois, USA: Tyndale House Publishers, 2004.

Bills, Taylor, Pat Schwiebert and Chuck DeKlyen. *Tear Soup*. Portland, Oregon, USA: Grief Watch, 2001.

Bloomfield, Harold H., M.D. & Peter McWilliams . *How to Survive the Loss of a Loved One.* Ingleburn, Australia: Prelude Press, 1991.

Buchanan, Mark. *Things Unseen.* New York, New York, USA: The Doubleday Religious Publishing Group, 2006.

Burnham, Gracia. To Fly Again: Surviving the tailspins of Life. Carol Stream, Illinois, USA: Tyndale House Publishers, 2005.

Calkin, Ruth Harms. "Release." *The One Year Book of Bible Promises.* Wheaton, Ill., USA: Tyndale House Publishers, Inc., 2000.

Curtis, Brent and John Eldridge. *The Sacred Romance.* Nashville, TN, USA: Thomas Nelson Inc., 1997.

Kent, Carol. A *New Kind of Normal.* Nashville, TN, USA: Thomas Nelson Inc., 2007.

Kent, Carol. N*ow I Lay My Isaac Down.* Colorado Springs, CO, USA: NavPress, 2004.

Mitsch, Raymond and Lynn Brookside. *Grieving the Loss of Someone You Love.* Ventura, California, USA: Gospel Light Publications, 1993.

Neufeldt, Elsie K. D*ancing in the Dark.* Vancouver, BC, Canada: Ronsdale Press, 1990.

Omartian, Stormie. *Just Enough Light for the Step I'm On.* Waterville, Maine, USA: Thorndike Press, 2004.

Peterson, Eugene. T*he Message: The Bible in Contemporary Language.* Colorado Springs: NavPress, 2002.

Shaughnessy, Susan Leigh. W*alking on Alligators: A book of Meditations for Writers.* San Francisco, CA, USA: Harper Collins Publishers, 1993.

Sittser, Jerry. A *Grace Disguised.* Grand Rapids, Michigan, USA: Zondervan, 2004.

Smith, Harold Ivan. A *Decembered Grief.* Kansas City, Kansas, USA: Beacon Hill Press, 1999.

Yancy, Phillip. D*isappointment with God.* Grand Rapids, Michigan, USA: Zondervan, 1992.

Yancy, Phillip. *Where is God When it Hurts?* Grand Rapids, Michigan, USA: Zondervan, 2002.

Young, Paul. T*he Shack.* Newbury Park, California, USA: Windblown Media, 2008.

Webster Dictionary, School Edition

Excerpts from *Our Daily Bread Devotional.* Grand Rapids, MI.

Good News Testament

Today's English Version Second Edition 1992 TEV

Contemporary English Version® CEV

MUSIC and POETRY

Bell, Steve. *Remember Me.* Rhythm House Records, Beyond a Shadow, 1999.

Foster, Ruthie. *Hole in My Pocket.* Tori Hendrix. Blue Corn Music, Runaway Soul, 2005.

Foster, Ruthie. *Walk On* Brownie McGhee. Blue Corn Music, Runaway Soul, 2005.

Foster, Ruthie. *Heal Yourself, Smalltown Blues, The Fight,* *M.O.D* Records, Full Circle, 1997.

Grant, Amy. *Breath of Heaven* (Mary's Song), Chris Eaton, Sparrow Records, Home For Christmas, 1992

Mullins, Rich. *Hard to Get. The* Jesus Record. Word Entertainment 1998

McCartney, Paul. Lennon, John. *Yesterday.*

Nordeman, Nichole. *You Are Good.* Sparrow Records, Sing Over Me, 2006.

Womack, Lee Ann. I *Hope You Dance.* MCA Nashville, UMG Recordings, 1997.

Holmes, Ernest. *"She Let Go."*

I initially encountered this poem in Australia at a writing workshop, and it was attributed to Ernest Holmes, I have discovered that the same poem is also credited to Rev. Safire Rose and to a Jennifer Eckert Bernau. (Some of the lines have been omitted in this account)

Lightning Source UK Ltd.
Milton Keynes UK
UKOW04f1129110917

308968UK00001B/115/P